Gods, Heroes, and Us
Greek Myths in the Modern Era

James Sale

© James Sale

Published in 2025 by The Bruges Group

Front and Back Cover by Linda E. Sale

ISBN: 978-1-917743-02-0

The Bruges Group Publications Office
246 Linen Hall, 162-168 Regent Street, London W1B 5TB
www.brugesgroup.com

Bruges Group publications are not intended to represent a corporate view of European and international developments. Contributions are chosen on the basis of their intellectual rigour, and their ability to open up new avenues for debate.

Scan me for Bruges Group

Twitter @brugesgroup, LinkedIn @brugesgroup
GETTR @brugesgroup, Telegram t.me/brugesgroup, Facebook @brugesgroup
Instagram @brugesgroup, YouTube @brugesgroup

Dedication

For the artist Linda E. Sale, my true Penelope, my true North, and to whom I am always returning.

Contents

Introduction	1
1. The Supremacy of Zeus in the Order of the Cosmos	9
2. Hubris and Apollo	20
3 Hubris and Hermes	31
4. Wisdom and Athene	40
5. Athene Helps: Perseus and Herakles	49
6. Orpheus and Eurydice and the Descent into Hell	59
7. Two Cautionary Tales – Midas and Narcissus	67
8. Truth and her Twin: Mendacium	77
9. Apollo, Mnemosyne and Poetry	71
10. Kairos and Pandora: Luck and Hope	95
11. Odysseus: Hero for today and journey of the soul	104
12. Odysseus and the Enneagram	117
Conclusion	130
Acknowledgements	135
About the Author	136
Other Books by James Sale	137
Reviews	138
Index	140

Introduction

It might be thought how strange it is that an organisation like The Bruges Group is publishing a work on Greek Myths, which perhaps seem distant, archaic and irrelevant to modern political, sociological and cultural concerns; exactly the concerns that concern The Bruges Group! However, the truth is that the Greek myths have never been more relevant. Why? Contrary to the modernist, post-modernist view that 'truth' itself does not exist or is relative, or is simply culturally conditioned and we can make it whatever we want it to be, there is another view that certain 'truths' are true and remain true whichever society succeeds to replace another, and despite and whatever people in a given society decide they want to be true. For, let's face it, it's human nature to start configuring reality the way we want it to be rather than the way it is.

This point is made not just in the West but in many religions; the Chinese in their Tao Te Ching[1] put it this way: "**If one does not recognize the eternal, one falls into confusion and sin. If one recognizes the eternal, one becomes forbearing. Forbearance leads to justice. Justice leads to mastery. Mastery leads to Heaven. Heaven leads to Tao. Tao leads to duration. All one's life long one is not in danger.**" The 'eternal', of course, is that unchanging truth that we need to respect, reverence and align ourselves with if we are to have happy and joyous lives. As the Tao recognizes, not to do so is to fall into 'confusion and sin' – and, for all those 'Justice Warriors' out there, into injustice too!

To be clear, then, it is not just Greek myths that are repositories of 'truth', but many myths and religions across the world in various cultures contain vast swathes of 'truth'; it just so happens that the Western canon is replete with these stories from ancient Greece since so many poets, writers, artists and musicians have elaborated on them precisely because of their 'truth', and so of their beauty and power. For this reason – their familiarity – and because of my love for them, I wish to explain some of the hidden or lesser-known insights, often psychological, of these Greek myths and show how they cast light on today's world, culture and values. As we will see, they frequently flatly contradict the value systems that are increasingly gripping our culture today, and as a result, we are falling into confusion, sin, injustice and shorter lives[2]. To quote one more time from the Tao Te Ching, we learn that: "**In leading

---

[1] *Tao Te Ching*, translation by Richard Wilhelm, 1985.
[2] In the United Kingdom, life expectancy has experienced fluctuations in recent years. Historically, there was a consistent increase in life expectancy throughout the 20th century, largely due to advancements in healthcare, improved living conditions, and public health initiatives. However, since 2011, the rate of increase has slowed, and in some periods, life expectancy has declined.

Men and in the service of Heaven, there is nothing better than 'Limitation'. For only through limitation can one deal with things early on." Limitation, as we shall see, is baked into the Greek myths, and perhaps its most potent expression is its concept of 'hubris': human beings are limited by a higher power which they disregard at their own peril.

There is another reason to explore Greek myths which is connected to what myths are in themselves. Karen Armstrong in her wonderfully short and helpful book[3] explains it like this: "A myth, it will be recalled, is an event that - in some sense - happened once, but which also happens all the time." This is an antidote to any sense in which myths or mythology is inferior to facts or what we call history. Of course, history is important; as Santayana[4] once observed, "Those who cannot remember the past are condemned to repeat it." However, myths may have occurred once, but even if they didn't, they are recurring all the time, which is why they speak to us. An example I like to use of this is one of the oldest and most familiar myths of all: the Fall in the Garden of Eden. Whether there was a literal Adam who fell or not (keeping in mind that the name Adam simply means Man – and Eve simply means Mother) is in one sense beside the point; for what we consistently observe is that mankind is 'falling' all the time. And even atheists[5] acknowledge this: "We inherit from Greek philosophy the belief that knowledge is liberating, but the biblical myth of the Fall is closer to the truth."

Yes, surprisingly, the 'myth' is closer to the truth! And John Gray goes on to say that "What none of the thinkers of the Enlightenment envisaged, and their followers today have failed to perceive, is that human life can become more savage and irrational even as scientific advance accelerates". Surely, this rings a bell? We have become more savage and more irrational even as 'scientific advance accelerates'? Which leads to his fundamental attack on the 'belief in progress' that prevents us perceiving evils: "Whatever role it may have had in the past, belief in progress has become a mechanism of self-deception that serves only to block perception of the evils that come with the growth of knowledge." Put another way, it prevents us from seeing the truth of our condition and what to do about it. Here, this book posits, is the value of Greek mythology; this alternative approach to understanding the world.

But before we get to exploring specific myths, we need to understand a little bit more about what has been going on historically. To begin with, it was a slow trickle in the Seventeenth century, accelerated in the Eighteenth with the advent of the Enlightenment, and then in the Twentieth and Twenty-First

---

[3] Karen Armstrong: *A short history of myth*, 2005.
[4] George Santayana, *The Life of Reason*, 1905.
[5] John Gray, *Heresies*, 2004.

centuries became a tsunami threatening to overwhelm our civilization entirely in its consequences. What am I talking about? The fact that we no longer – unlike our predecessors – see myths as living, as instructive, and as meaningful. Our dictionaries now attest to the fossilized fact that the word 'myth' is more or less synonymous with make-belief.

In the Shorter Oxford English Dictionary myth is "a purely fictitious narrative"; and elsewhere we find that it is "a commonly-held belief that is untrue, or without foundation"; these kinds of definitions can be replicated in all dictionaries. The 'fact' is that myth now is commonly understood to mean: a story which is untrue, but which we like anyway, because we like stories! Indeed, the origin of the word myth is from a Greek word meaning fable or narrative.

There are two important points to grasp here: first, as we have already noted, that being a myth, therefore, is not important because it is untrue, non-factual, imaginary; and two, that by implication real knowledge is in another domain, and we call that domain 'science'. If this seems academic, then we need to think again, for the consequences of these beliefs, even if subconscious, are quite profound: we see it in our educational systems as mathematics and sciences are increasingly predicated as more important than the humanities and arts, and so the funding increasingly goes one way and not the other; we see it in the respect accorded to the science and technologies, whereas the arts – accepting the relatively few Hollywood stars and multi-platinum artists – are the poor relations; and in the UK, and to a lesser extent in the USA, the term poet is almost a term of contempt – mainstream takes barely any notice of poets at all!

But reality is very different. For, as Professor Brian Cox[6] once sagely observed, "narrative may be regarded as a primary act of mind". We can only understand reality through story. Even science has to revert to narrative (or is that fable, or myth?) to explain itself. Take its most famous narrative: The Big Bang! What is that? But a story, which the human mind *gets*. Of course, being scientists, they like to 'imagine' that because scientists say so, it must be true, or a true story, although even to a casual observer the story – for example, the time frame – seems to change as it progresses. That, though, is explained – conveniently - by the word 'progress', to which we shall return again shortly.

Myth is not a fiction in the sense that it is untrue, but a story in which profound truth is communicated or embodied. In fact, the most important truths of all are conveyed via myths. What are these truths that are so profound, and why are we not aware of them? First, we are not aware because we have lost the capacity to see

---

[6] Brian Cox, *The Cox Report*, 1989.

them; and the truths themselves are invisible. That's right – they are invisible; all of the most important things in the world are invisible when we actually think about it. Thinking itself, incidentally, is also invisible: we can't see 'thinking' except perhaps in our mind's eye – which is where the important, the deep truths lie. To give examples: what is more important than 'love', or 'goodness', or 'ideas' or our 'values', but none of these things are visible, and yet we can easily die for them. And of utmost importance, beyond the invisibilities already mentioned, are, in the Western tradition, God, and in the Eastern one, the Tao. The Tao in the first line of the Tao Te Ching goes beyond even invisibility, for it says, 'The Tao that can be spoken of is not the eternal Tao'. Invisible? Inaudible and mute too.

Thus, myths are making the invisible visible, so that we as humans can understand more readily what reality – the Tao, the nature of God – is like, and so modify our being and behaviour accordingly in order to avoid what the Greeks called hubris. Hubris is what destroys us – so, yes, it is important to be able to understand myth, for our own future depends on it. The Ancient Egyptian Book of the Dead said, "All the world which lies below has been set in order and filled in contents by the things which are placed above; for the things below have not the power to set in order the world above". A clear reminder of mortality and of human nature and its limitations.

So let us return to a myth I have already mentioned to help make clearer what I am saying. You will recall in the Garden of Eden that there were two trees: the Tree of Knowledge and the Tree of Life. Sadly, man reached out and chose the Tree of Knowledge. What does that mean? Man reached out and chose facts, data, certainty, or the visible over the Tree of Life, which was the imaginative, the trusting, the uncertain, or the invisible. But what is made clear in the story is that that choice – of knowledge – is death. The word 'science' itself etymologically means 'knowledge' and who could actually deny that the whole planet now is precariously lurching towards its own self-generated Armageddon derived from science – the knowledge that has polluted the planet, invented biological and atomic weaponry, and much more beside. As the USA and North Korea and Russia, not to mention China, sabre-rattle in their different ways (and this is not to allocate blame) don't we feel the danger the whole world is in?

The irony is that science has generated its own myths (although it can't accept its views are myths) to perpetuate its own supremacy, and so avoid genuine scrutiny and accountability. The most pernicious of these is the myth it has of 'progress'. The Ancients believed we had a Golden Age in the past; but the moderns discard all that – superstition! – for the Golden Age is coming. Ever coming, but never arriving, of course. So, alongside the 'progress' of science, we have 'progressive' politics too, which has come to mean let's allow people to do whatever they want – aka, general anarchy - and do-whatever, physically, mentally, morally[7]; and we also have a fatuous progressive history of the world that presupposes things are getting better despite the evidence of two World Wars and horrors on a scale never dreamt of before. Even Alexander the Great or Genghis Khan would have been impressed by the savagery and destruction wrought by men who all shared the concept of 'progress', 'wars to end all wars', and 'never again'.

And in case we have not yet got the connection with myth, and the seriousness of failing to understand myth, consider one example: what happened in the Soviet Union? And where did their pernicious ideas come from? From Karl Marx[8], a man who couldn't and wouldn't understand myth. So, when faced with the Biblical injunction, 'man shall not live by bread alone', facetiously suggested that though he may not be able to live by bread alone, man cannot exist without bread. That was his 'fact', that was his Tree of Knowledge – and not seeing either the inner meaning of the expression, that merely to live economically is to live like an animal, for that is all animals do, which is to deny our humanity, or that this was a call from Moses[9] (who 'trusted Him who is invisible' – again, that concept) to a new way of living. As we know, like humanity in Eden, the Israelites failed to heed Moses' warning. The rest is history.

The consequences of failing to heed or understand myth, then, are profound, and I would like to explore some myths and draw out for you some implications for our understanding of the modern world and what this means for us. There are 12 chapters in the book and the ordering starts not at the actual beginning but at what I perceive as the real beginning: namely, the establishment of order through the supremacy of Zeus. This order is in a sense what we referred to earlier when we talked of 'limitation'; to order is to limit. Before the 'limiting' the cosmos was chaotic and totally disordered; indeed, it was a dog-eat-dog world where might was/is right. But with the coming of Zeus order was established, which meant also law and justice. I say more about these topics in the first chapter, but for now that this 'ordering' is a central issue of our times: everywhere we look in the UK (and the West generally), we find disorder going on. Why?

---

[7] The only caveat to this general advocation of promiscuity in morality is the weak qualification: 'so long as you don't hurt anybody else.'
[8] From Marx's "Economic and Philosophic Manuscripts of 1844," where he discusses human needs and alienation. Marx's focus on materialism led him to critique the biblical notion that "man shall not live by bread alone," suggesting that, in reality, without bread (i.e., basic material sustenance), human existence is untenable.
[9] Moses' faith is described in the Hebrews 11:27: "By faith he left Egypt, not fearing the wrath of the king; for he endured, as seeing Him who is unseen." (NASB)

Ordering implies hierarchy; and this – hierarchy - the progressives, the revolutionaries and the 'justice warriors' of the West detest and cannot abide. It seems to stand four-square against their concepts of equality and equity. However, as Jordan B Peterson[10] said, "…the dominance hierarchy, however social or cultural it might appear, has been around for some half a billion years. It's permanent. It's real. The dominance hierarchy is not capitalism, it's not communism, either … it's not even patriarchy … it is instead a near-eternal aspect of the environment, and much of what is blamed on these more ephemeral manifestations is a consequence of its unchanging existence … Dominance hierarchies are older than trees." In short, it's immoveable, and all efforts to undo it are in vain. The Greek myth of Zeus makes this really clear.

And following from it, we look at the cardinal sin of human beings from the Greek perspective: hubris. Hubris is essentially when human beings violate their limitations and bring disorder to the world by doing so. Two chapters explore this in relation to two specific gods, Apollo and Hermes. But from there and the dastardly consequences of hubris we move to my favourite goddess, Athene, and in two chapters explicate her wisdom and how she uses it to help two 'human' heroes, Perseus and Herakles. I say human because at this point in the Greek mythology, both Perseus and Herakles (who is incidentally also Perseus' great grandson) are semi-human or semi-divine, since both are fathered by Zeus; and in that sense they represent – through the agency of his daughter, Athene – the continuation of his work in Heaven to produce order, here on Earth.

At this juncture, chapter 6, we have reached the midpoint of the book, so it seems appropriate to focus on another type of hero: Perseus is a hero who symbolizes cleverness and resourcefulness, whereas Herakles embodies strength and endurance; now we consider Orpheus, the poet and singer, and the ultimate challenge he faces for all mortals – the descent into Hell. Hell is important to understand because it is the place where all that is not ordered is consigned forever. And, as Colonel Percy Harrison Fawcett[11] once noted, "The exit from Hell is always difficult". Possibly an understatement[12]!

After Hell we consider two famous myths: that of Midas and Narcissus, and we learn how their activities are hellish, hubristic, and highly relevant to our world today. As is the lesser-known myth of Mendacium, from which we get our own word, mendacity: to lie.

---

[10] Jordan B Peterson, *12 Rules for Life*, 2018.
[11] Quoted in the book, *The Lost City of Z*, David Grann, 2009.
[12] Not only Colonel Harrington commented on its difficulty: "It is easy to descend into Avernus. Death's dark door stands open day and night. But to retrace your steps and get back to upper air, that is the task, that is the undertaking." - Virgil Aeneid 6. 126-129, translated by Seamus Heaney.

How difficult it is to distinguish between truth and lies. This myth gives us some important clues.

We return in chapter 9 to my favourite Greek god, Apollo. Earlier in chapter 2 we saw his role in punishing hubris, but Apollo is the god of much more than that: of light – of prophecy, which follows from the 'seeing' accorded by light – of poetry, an ultimate ordering of sound – and so of healing, which comes from the ordered mind and body. Now we consider Apollo's role in the creation of poetry. A corrective perhaps to its modern abandonment in the West.

In chapter 10 we visit another relatively obscure and unknown god, at least to the non-specialists in Greek mythology: Kairos. Essentially, the god of time, but time understood as the right moment, seizing the right moment; and from that of course, we derive 'luck'. Also, this is a good moment – the right moment! – to pair this myth with the well-known one of Pandora, who is essentially, of course, the Greek Myth equivalent to Eve in the Garden of Eden: the woman through whom the woes of the world were released. But again, we must not forget what was left: hope.

Finally, we devote the last two chapters to the most famous Greek hero of all, and the most famous world epic of all: Odysseus and the Odyssey. It is very strange that Odysseus should be so famous, and that I should even rank him above Herakles, whom many – perhaps with some justification – might think of as a greater hero. He was stronger than Odysseus, he stormed Hell, rather than sipped at its fringes as Odysseus did, his exploits were certainly as incredible and various as Odysseus's, and in the twelve Labours we have, as it were, heavenly aspirations to match the constellations of the zodiac. Incredible! Perhaps another book will say more about all this, but the thing is: Herakles was a demi-god, whereas Odysseus, coming at the end of the heroic tradition – the Golden Age of Herakles giving way to the Bronze Age of Achilles (descended from the immortal nymph, Thetis) and finally with Odysseus, the last of the Bronze Age warriors, the Iron Age of mere men is arriving and has arrived. The greatness of Odysseus is just that: he has no immortal pedigree; he is just a man.

And that is why, over the ages, so many have identified with him: he is *us* – no super strength, no super powers, no super weapons, but just a trained warrior relying on his cunning and his wits. In this way, then, we can identify with him; and so can - and has - our Western culture over three millennia. The Odyssey has become synonymous with our own journey 'home'.

Therefore, let me invite you now to explore these myths again, or even for the first time, and see for yourself what profound teachings they contain for all us if we can but learn afresh what deep within us, we have always known. Remember that if we ignore these teachings, then they will return – as we said myths do (for myths happen all the time); as Jung[13] disturbingly observed – "what we have ignored or denied inwardly will then more likely come to us as outer fate." And does this warning remind us of a Greek myth, one we have not dealt with specifically in this book? Yes, indeed it does: Oedipus, who to avoid his fate went out of his way to ensure that it could never happen, but in doing so fulfilled it.

There is, in short, to quote James Hollis[14] again: "A mystery so profound that none of us really seems to grasp it until it has indisputably grasped us, is that some force transcendent to ordinary consciousness is at work within us to bring about our ego's overthrow." Unless we in the West accept the mysteries and the myths – words etymologically related – we are all destined to meet that nemesis we so desperately seek to avoid.

Again[15]: "How could this be, that we could be our own enemy? They [the Greeks] understood that there were forces in the cosmos to which even the gods were subject. Such forces they named Moirai, or 'fate', sophrosyne, or 'what goes around comes around', dike, or 'justice', nemesis, or 'consequential retribution', and pro erasmus, 'destiny'. These forces might be translated by us today as the organizing, balancing, structuring powers of the cosmos, a word which itself means 'order'." That word again, 'order' – where we start in chapter 1.

---

[13] Cited in James Hollis, *Finding Meaning in the Second Half of Life*, 2006.
[14] James Hollis, ibid.
[15] James Hollis, ibid.

Chapter 1:
The Supremacy of Zeus in the Order of the Cosmos

Why does existence exist? This question is not a scientific question, since science cannot answer it. But it is a question that all major religions of the world have a view on; it is in essence a spiritual question. What major religions today think about why existence exists is not the purpose of this book to discuss, but the ancient world, and especially the Greeks – paganism if you will – certainly wanted to account for the origins of things, and in doing so provided a rationale for the existence of all that is.

According to Hesiod and other sources, before existence commenced, there was Chaos, which was a vast, dark void of primordial emptiness. Within that Gaia – the Earth – emerged as the foundation for all existence, although the Earth within herself contained Tartarus, a gloomy abyss. Eros (Love) also came into being as a force of attraction, and this led to Chaos giving birth to Erebus (Darkness) and Nyx (Night). Erebus and Nyx coupled and produced offspring such as Air and Day, whilst Gaia's offspring included Uranus (Sky), Mountains and Sea.

At this point things become interesting: Gaia coupled with her own son, Uranus, to produce the Titans[16], the Cyclops[17] and the Hecatoncheires[18]. Gaia hated Uranus because he imprisoned some of their own children in Tartarus, so she enabled – with a sickle - one of her sons, the Titan, Cronus, to castrate his father and take control. But Cronus, after taking control of the Cosmos, treated his own sons no better than his father had: because a prophecy had said that one of his children would be greater than him, he ate them all! However, as they were immortal beings, the children he swallowed were not dead, and through a trick by which the youngest, Zeus, was not swallowed, he restored his brothers and sisters, and they returned to defeat Cronus and the Titans in battle,

So, this is the simplified backstory to the reign of Zeus as the supreme god over all the Earth and the Heavens too; in fact, of the whole cosmos. There are a couple of things to notice about this story. First, that before we arrive at Zeus, the cosmos is an extremely irregular, violent and random kind of place. Prior to the arrival of the Titans, we have plenty of chaos, darkness and gloom; with the Titans themselves, we seem to have primitive and elemental beings/forces that constantly strive for supremacy in what we now might call a survival of the fittest world. Admittedly

---

[16] The Titans were a race of powerful deities who preceded the Olympian gods. They were the children of Uranus (Sky) and Gaia (Earth).
[17] The Cyclops were one-eyed giants, also children of Uranus and Gaia.
[18] The Hecatoncheires, also called the "Hundred-Handed Ones," were monstrous beings with fifty heads and one hundred arms each.

Uranus is cruel, but he is castrated by his own son (the blood, incidentally from his wound, spurts into the sea and from the foam the goddess Aphrodite emerges); and the son, Cronus, eats his own children – a rather revolting form of cannibalism (of course, for Cronus understood symbolically as Time, this is appropriate since Time does eat all his children, literally from second to second). By contrast, when Cronus is defeated by Zeus, he is merely consigned to Tartarus where, impotent to do harm to the gods, he lives on.

Secondly, the enthronement of Zeus initiates a new order to the Cosmos: an order that is characterized by a number of features. The first and certainly most important feature is order itself, for what we have had before has been highly disordered. Zeus creates and sustains order – and order has several consequences: it means law, justice, and hierarchy to mention just three items. And a fourth would be peace, for in bringing the Titanomachy (the war against Cronus and his fellow Titans to an end) peace is established, and with peace comes stability. The Cosmos can now look forward to a period of calm, peace and stability, flourishing under such conditions.

But here's the thing about creating this order: Zeus in doing so becomes NOT an absolute monarch (or Tyrant), although he has supreme power, but he too is bound by the laws of his own order. He himself, for example, cannot violate an oath solemnly undertaken (and binding when sworn over the River Styx). He, too, cannot violate Fate (called in Greek mythology The Moirai) and this includes his inability to override prophecies even when they concern him. Finally, Zeus cannot change the fundamental laws of nature and the cycles of life and death. Zeus, then, is very much a part of, and involved with, the creation and the Cosmos; the word 'cosmos' itself means 'order' or 'orderly arrangement'. Thus, we may well understand his importance both in psychological and as well as moral terms.

And how is all this relevant to today's world? Well, in mentioning psychology and Zeus, Jung expressed it this way: "We think we can congratulate ourselves on having already reached such a pinnacle of clarity, imagining that we have left all these phantasmal gods far behind. But what we have left behind are only verbal spectres, not the psychic facts that were responsible for the birth of the gods. We are still as much possessed today by autonomous psychic contents as if they were Olympians. Today they are called phobias, obsessions, and so forth; in a word, neurotic symptoms. The gods have become diseases; Zeus no longer rules Olympus but rather the solar plexus, and produces curious specimens for the doctor's consulting room, or disorders the brains of politicians and journalists who unwittingly let loose psychic epidemics on the world." Whether we agree exactly with Jung's prognosis or not is immaterial: what is important in this chapter is what the existence of the gods and their mythology tells us about what is essential to the 'good' life. The 'good life' being, at an elementary level, or perhaps negative level, a life without phobias, obsessions and neurotic symptoms; what it means on a positive level, we shall consider shortly.

Thus, we have six points that emerge from creation of the Cosmos that are critical: order, law, justice, hierarchy, peace and stability. If we think about these six things and contrast them with our society in the West, what do we find? We find, in fact, that in every one of these specifics, we are lacking its substance and so – consequently – heading for the Chaos that was there in the beginning. Let's consider each item in a little more detail.

1. Order

Order is such a vital aspect of the Greek myths: it was for this that the new gods prevailed. And we need to keep in mind that all the great spiritual traditions continually uphold and emphasize this pivotal role of order, and so of meaning. Two examples would be the opening verses of the gospel of St John and its concept of the Logos[19]; and the whole thrust of the Tao Che Ching and the role of the Tao in ordering our lives[20]. But the pagans saw it too. The whole point of Zeus's fight with the Titans and afterwards the Giants was to sustain the order – the meaning – of the cosmos. If Cronus, or subsequently Typhon, had prevailed against Zeus, the universe would have slid into chaos – which is to say, meaninglessness.

Notice that there has to be a 'fight' for this order; there seems to be a constant tendency for the forces of disorder to overtake and destroy order. This is a theme will shall come back to, as the victory of Zeus was never complete: pockets, offspring, contaminations of evil – typically as monsters – continue to wreck the world, and the semi-divine heroes (Herakles, son of Zeus, most spectacularly) are sent to clean up the mess that continually arises.

But let's be clear that order and meaning go hand in hand. The great anthropologist, Claude Levi-Strauss, expressed it this way in his book on "Myth": "It is, I think, absolutely impossible to conceive of meaning without order... The common denominator [of all human intellectual undertakings] is always to introduce some kind of order. If this represents a basic need for order in the human

---

[19] St John's gospel begins with: "In the beginning was the Word, and the Word was with God, and the Word was God." The Greek word for 'Word' is Logos and it also means 'meaning'; thus, in the beginning was the meaning ...
[20] As we said in the Introduction, limitation is what creates order: "In leading Men and in the service of Heaven
There is nothing better than 'Limitation'. For only through limitation Can one deal with things early on" – Tao Te Ching, Richard Wilhelm translation.

mind and since, after all, the human mind is only part of the universe, the need probably exists because there is some order in the universe and the universe is not a chaos."

This statement has tremendous implications. CS Lewis commented that "If the whole universe has no meaning, we should never have found out that it has no meaning: just as, if there were no light in the universe and therefore no creatures with eyes, we should never know it was dark. Dark would be meaningless." Based on Levi-Strauss' observation we [21] could equally well substitute the word 'order' for meaning, for they are clearly virtually synonymous here.

What the myth, then, clearly tells us is that postmodernism, subjectivism, and materialism (three major '-isms' of our time) are wrong. Why? Because they posit, at root, meaninglessness as the basis for our observations of the natural world and wider universe: they presuppose no truth (postmodernism), no objectivity (subjectivity) and no purpose (materialism) in the universe and in our lives. Contrary to supposing these negative qualities, the Ancient Greeks presuppose order, which itself implies a seventh quality we have not yet mentioned: beauty. We will look at this issue in more depth in chapter 9.

2. Law

Following on from the notion that Zeus and the Olympian gods established order, comes the idea of law. There are various kinds of law (which is essentially, a codified order) – each in its own domain. So, they believed in natural law, that the cosmos was governed by them, and this led to their scientific and philosophical enquiries. Also, social laws were necessary, ideally to reflect the natural order and so establish harmony. They also focused on political laws – hence the rich flowering of various government models, including democracy; they focused on philosophical and mathematical laws – Plato, Aristotle, Pythagoras et al establishing rational principles on which to develop their works. Artistic laws – in rhetoric and architecture; legal 'laws', as in Draco's code or Solon's reforms in Athens to lay the foundations for a fair and orderly society.

In short, the story of Zeus establishing order in the cosmos had profound implications in how and what they believed about that cosmos and how applicable it all was to life on Earth. For ultimately, (though of course not all Greeks believed in the myths) underpinning all the laws were divine laws. These divine laws were

---

[21] An acceptance of the world as a divinely ordered cosmos wherein everything is given a meaning is neither self-contradictory nor inconsistent with empirical knowledge, and yet it can never be a consequence of such knowledge, however vastly expanded - Leszek Kolakowski, Religion, p 50.

in essence moral. Zeus, for example, particularly emphasized the duty of hospitality to guests and strangers (a principle known as xenia): to commit a crime against a guest in your house was considered to be an especially heinous crime which would invoke severe retribution from Zeus himself in the form of curses, disasters, or direct intervention. This divine law has been seriously eroded in the West, but we see vestiges of it in Shakespeare's play, "Macbeth": the treachery of Macbeth is not just that he had sworn allegiance to King Duncan, or even that he was a kinsman – the equal, possibly greater sin was that he was murdering him when he was a guest in his own home. This Macbeth himself acknowledges[22].

Another of these divine (or moral) laws is the law of hubris, which we look at in more detail in chapter 2. Three other laws are given by Apollo: Know Thyself, Nothing in Excess and Surety Brings Ruin – these laws are really an extension or examples, re-statements of the hubris law as we shall see and explore.

What is the relevance of this today? Well, we live in a world in which being an anarchist, being a 'progressive', being a 'culture-warrior' is seen as not only acceptable (a badge of honour in fact) but somehow morally superior to what ordinary people perceive as right, proper and lawful. But in essence these three types are more about the removal of laws, the abolition of constraints, and the more general disconnection between cause and effect, action and consequence, appearance and reality, than they are about living in peace with others. Indeed, because they project moral superiority, they hold themselves above the law or laws that are appertain to other people. Again, this is a form of hubris which violates the divine order; and there is an accountability which will follow, for as Ayn Rand[23] noted: "We can ignore reality, but we cannot ignore the consequences of ignoring reality".

3. Justice or Dike

The Greeks had a specific goddess for justice: Dike (or sometimes written Diké). She was the daughter of Zeus and Themis (a Titaness also associated with the laws of nature). Our own concept of 'blind' justice, of weighing the scales of justice, derives from her nature. In Greek philosophy, particularly in the works of Plato, Dike represents cosmic justice and moral order. And in Hesiod, she is associated with the Golden Age of mankind when man lived in harmony with the gods and there was peace on Earth. Indeed,

---

[22] "He's here in double trust:
First, as I am his kinsman and his subject,
Strong both against the deed; then, as his host,
Who should against his murderer shut the door,
Not bear the knife myself." - Macbeth, Act 1, Scene 7
[23] Ayn Rand, *Atlas Shrugged*, 1957.

Hesiod describes how morality declined in the world, so Dike retreated from the Earth to go and live with the gods. She is seen as the star sign Virgo in the zodiac.

This idea of morality weakening and thereby creating a retreat of justice sounds all too familiar to today's world, doesn't it? The adoption of philosophical positions such as the three we have mentioned - postmodernism, subjectivism, and materialism – must, as night follows days – lead to a diminution of justice; for, as we abandon the notion of divine and moral law, we find that our notion of justice weakens; it weakens because it becomes entirely 'subjective'. That word again! A million subjectivities, a billion *Likes* on X (Twitter) or Facebook does not constitute anything remotely resembling justice. Rather, justice becomes – today - more like a Roman Amphitheatre where thumbs-up or thumbs-down determines outcomes in an irrational (that is, in a populist, non-ordered) way.

So that, from the West, serious crimes (e.g. murder) come to be seen less and less as serious crimes: many of the perpetrators are no longer responsible for their actions: social factors (e.g. poverty) are to blame, psychological difficulties (e.g. depression) are invoked, and theories of remediation are proffered whereby the aim is less about punishing the offender but more about rehabilitating them.

Alongside, then, the weakening of culpability, comes the weakening of the sentencing, or punishments doled out. The abolition of capital punishment is all but an invention of the modern West. It may seem strange now, because we have all absorbed the meme that capital punishment is barbaric, but there are scarcely any societies in the past that did not practise it[24]. And even when small pockets of civilization – such as Athens in the 5th century BC – did abolish it temporarily, there were still exceptions made: for example, non-citizens could be executed.

---

[24] i. Ancient Greece: While capital punishment was used in many Greek city-states, Ancient Athens during certain periods (particularly in the 5th century BCE) had largely abolished it for citizens. The philosopher Plato argued against its use in his work "Laws."
ii. Kievan Rus: In the 11th century, Yaroslav the Wise introduced a legal code called the Russkaya Pravda, which abolished capital punishment and instead focused on fines and reconciliation.
iii. Medieval Iceland (930-1262 CE): The Old Icelandic Commonwealth did not have an executive branch of government and didn't use capital punishment. Their legal system was based on compensation and outlawry.
iv. Tokugawa Japan (1603-1868): While capital punishment existed, it was used sparingly compared to contemporary European nations. Many crimes were punished by exile or fines instead.
v. San Marino: This small European republic abolished the death penalty for civil crimes in 1848, though it remained for military crimes until 1865.
vi. Some Native American tribes: Certain indigenous North American societies, such as the Iroquois Confederacy, often used restorative justice practices rather than capital punishment.
vii. Bhutan: This Himalayan kingdom did not have capital punishment for much of its history, formally abolishing it in 2004.

It is interesting that when capital punishment was abolished in the UK in 1965[25], one of the important conditions of its abolition was that 'life would mean life': that a life sentence was not going to be an easy option for the perpetrators of serious crime. This was a rhetorical concession or flourish made by the abolitionists to help push through the law in the face of the opposition who claimed that murderers would otherwise get away with murder! Very quickly, however, once the death penalty had been removed, the 'life sentences' came to mean a long stretch, then a less long stretch, and then finally – with good behaviour – one could be out in half the sentence! What was once a hanging offence became, typically in the UK, sixteen years in prison and then release – sometimes to murder again!

That said, we ought to note that as various criminal sentences are reduced for real crimes, currently they can be very different for 'invented' crimes such as 'hate speech'. So, in the UK, for example, shop-lifting, burglary[26], knife crime et al. seem not to be crimes at all; at least in the sense that they are hardly dealt with by the police; but Julie Sweeney[27], a "quiet 53-year old wife from Cheshire", described as a 'keyboard' warrior' posts on Facebook and is sentenced to 15 months in prison: her post was inflammatory and abhorrent, but is it 'justice' when the so-called 'full force of the law' is thrown at her, but not at shop-lifters, burglars and those carrying knives? Indeed, the current UK Prime Minister[28] has been designated 'Two-Tier-Kier' as a result of public perception of these varying policing and legal situations.

More generally, what we have reached is the point, almost, where crime is no longer a crime, but is considered and treated as an illness or disease – something requiring treatment, but nothing punitive in nature; everybody can be 'saved', and utopia is possible. And as a sidebar on this issue: it is interesting to note that the traditional beliefs in hell, which are almost universal[29], have also weakened: forms of universalism reign – nobody goes to hell anymore! That would be 'judgmental', which is for some the worst

---

[25] The abolition began in 1965 through The Murder (Abolition of the Death Penalty) Act which abolished capital punishment for murder in Great Britain, replacing it with life imprisonment. The death penalty remained in place for high treason, piracy with violence, arson in royal dockyards, and espionage, until these punishments too were changed.

[26] To take just burglary, in the UK: there were 266,489 recorded burglary offences in England and Wales in the year ending March 2024, and only about 4.3% of burglary cases led to a charge or summons in the year ending March 2024.

[27] https://www.telegraph.co.uk/news/2024/08/14/judge-jails-keyboard-warrior-over-blow-up-mosque-post/

[28] https://www.telegraph.co.uk/news/2024/11/05/from-policing-to-tax-keir-is-two-tier-on-everything/

[29] The Greeks believed in the afterlife and hell, as did Virgil in his Aeneid. The Ancient Egyptians also believed in it; and if we come up to date even the most 'compassionate' or so-called tolerant of religions, Buddhism, believes in it, for what else is reincarnation except a perpetual form of hell?

crime of all. As Theodore Dalrymple [30] expressed it: "When young people want to praise themselves, they describe themselves as 'non-judgmental'. For them, the highest form of morality is amorality." Dike, then, is in retreat, has left the Earth, and has retired to the constellation of Virgo!

4. Hierarchy

Here the Greek myths are very emphatic: the whole point – in one sense – of Zeus' victory was for him to become top dog, to become the apex of the Cosmos, and from him all authority flowed down. First, the twelve Olympian gods became effectively the ruling council of the universe with Zeus as their head; one god, Hades, did not participate in the rulings of the twelve, but had his own domain (called Hades or Hell) which no-one had better mess with: Aesculapius tried (by raising someone from the dead) and Zeus soon demolished him with a lightning bolt.

This action by Zeus demonstrates the connection between order and hierarchy. Essentially, by attempting to raise the dead through his medical powers, Aesculapius was not only depriving Hades of another 'subject' in his kingdom, but was also subverting the natural order, which is that humans have to die: order and law require that it is forbidden for a man to exceed this natural limit. Mankind is below the gods in the natural packing order, as it were.

But not only mankind. Beneath the gods were also other, lesser divine beings, including titans, river gods, nymphs, satyrs, fauns, cyclops, harpies, centaurs and so on. These beings interacted – not always consistently – in the myths with the gods and with humans. And humans themselves were not at the bottom of the natural order, for the Earth itself came under their jurisdiction, as they themselves were under the gods' jurisdiction.

Hierarchy, then, is critical to reality and the stability of the cosmos. But this idea of hierarchy is anathema to 'woke- warriors' and believers in IDE (Inclusion, Diversity, Equity). To take 'equity' as the overarching concept, Kenneth LaFave asks, 'where is the physical-world example of 'equity'? Where are two of anything the same? ... It can now be seen that the struggle between Right and Left is at its core a metaphysical conflict.'

I cited Jordan B. Peterson earlier on the prevalence of the dominance hierarchy, and that dominance hierarchies were 'older than trees'. More immediately, Jay Langdale[31] put it this way: 'If society is something which can be understood, it must have a structure; if it has structure, it must have hierarchy.' And not only contemporary thinkers, but the greatest writer in the English

---

[30] Theodore Dalrymple, *Our Culture, What's Left of It*, 2005.
[31] Jay Langdale, Remembering Richard Weaver, Chronicles, February 2020.

language, Shakespeare, knew it too through his character, Ulysses:

> 'Take but degree away, untune that string,
> And, hark, what discord follows. Each thing meets
> In mere oppugnancy. The bounded waters
> Should lift their bosoms higher than the shores
> And make a sop of all this solid globe…
> — Troilus and Cressida, Act 1 scene 3

Take 'degree' away – degree here means hierarchy – then we find discord follows: a musical metaphor following on from 'untune that string'; harmony is lost, which of course also means beauty is lost. Each thing meets – congregates – in 'mere oppugnancy': meaning hostility and resistance. In short, we find the world would return to the state that Zeus lifted it from when he defeated Cronus. And beyond people's conflicts, note how Shakespeare virtually predicts a second Noah's Flood – the solid globe becomes a sop – or the end of the world!

5. Peace

It should be quite clear by now that the breakdown of, the abandonment of, the clear principles of cosmic order, as established by Zeus, meaning order itself (and so meaning), law, justice (Dike), hierarchy leads not to peace but it's opposite as Shakespeare predicted, and as the whole Zeus mythology intimates.

Over and above the complete breakdown of society, the loss of peace means at least two distinct things: one, war and warfare; two, loss of peace of mind. This latter point is quite important too in today's increasingly broken society in which mental illnesses and breakdowns are massively on the rise, especially following the worldwide Covid-19 epidemic[32]. Peace of mind – leaving aside theological beliefs – is arguably the primary aim of all our endeavours, whether we know it or not.

So, an argument might be: what do you want? I want a successful career. Why? So that I can make money? Why? So that I can retire early? Why? So that I can enjoy life? Why? So that I can spend time with my loved ones. Why? So that I can feel that my time is well spent. Why? So that I can have … peace of mind, contentment, happiness … call it what you will, but after about 6

---

[32] For example, In the past year, 3.8 million people sought NHS mental health support, a substantial increase from 2.7 million in 2019: https://www.thescottishsun.co.uk/health/13901087/negative-online-content-mental-health-warning-study/?utm_source=chatgpt.com

Whys, we end up wanting peace. As Goethe[33] said, 'On all the peaks lies peace.'

As regards the peace that is the absence of war and warfare, there are two things to observe. First, that man is limited, but free, and so responsible for his actions even when he did not directly intend them: Oedipus did not intend to kill his father or marry his mother, but nevertheless did and was held responsible, and consequently paid for his actions. Second, as a result of that freedom, mankind is always being tempted to hubris: hubris has consequences individually and collectively. In the latter case, warfare becomes inevitable: Troy was rich and powerful – the Washington DC of its day. But it had become proud and its hubris had alienated at least three very important gods: Athene (goddess of wisdom and favourite offspring of Zeus) and Hera (wife of Zeus) were offended by the hubris of Paris[34] (as shown in his 'judgement'), son of the king of Troy, but the clinching issue was that in abducting Helen from Menelaus' palace when he was a guest there, Paris committed xenia against Zeus himself – he had betrayed the guest-host relationship. In defending his son's actions, Priam, king of Troy, therefore participated (on behalf of all Troy) in the hubris of his son and so he, and all the city, had to endure the inevitable punishment.

Hubris is an act that disturbs the order established by Zeus, and so must be punished: war in this sense, therefore, is necessary to restore peace – and so to restore stability.

6. Stability

Technically, I guess the opposite of stability is instability, and when we refer to things being unstable, what we mean is that they fall over, they break down, they cannot remain composed – that is, as it were, knit together and coherent. In short, once more disorder is occurring – the opposite of what Zeus intended when he took control.

Thus, what we would expect in a society that ignores divine mandates is an increasing amount of instability: civil unrest, injustice, hierarchical flattening, lawlessness, increasing crime rates, lack of respect for authorities, indiscipline and perhaps most crucially of all, family breakdown in which the veneration due to elders and senior members is either not forthcoming or actively discounted. A society, in other words, in which the children take

---

[33] On all the peaks lies peace" ("*Über allen Gipfeln ist Ruh*" in German) comes from his poem "Wanderer's Nightsong II" ("*Wandrers Nachtlied* II").

[34] The judgement of Paris meant rejecting the queen of the gods, Hera, and also rejecting Pallas Athene; instead of them, he declared Aphrodite, goddess of love and sex, as most beautiful; such a choice was disastrous for him and for his city of Troy, where his father, Priam, was king.

control and believe – profoundly - in their own wisdom and their own God-given entitlements; and naturally, discounting the wisdom of those who came before.

It is not for nothing that Zeus is called 'Father Zeus' – Homer refers to him as such, lyric poets like Pindar used this epithet, other gods refer to him as 'Father', and this epithet is found on ancient Greek coins, statues, and dedicatory inscriptions. Zeus, of course, had his own father, Cronus, but he was not a father of order and harmony, but part of the chaos that pre-existed the rule of Zeus. Cronus, therefore, is not a real father since he had not the seeds of order within him. By referring to Zeus as 'Father' we stipulate the importance of the father in all ordered family relationships (and, incidentally here, the importance of the male principle). Without the 'father' – and its hierarchy – the family would be asymmetrical, unbalanced, as it were, which means with a tendency to break down.

What we find in the West is just such a breakdown. To take just the issue of being fatherless, Edward Kruk[35] found that "71% of high school dropouts are fatherless; fatherless children have more trouble academically, scoring poorly on tests of reading, mathematics, and thinking skills; children from father-absent homes are more likely to be truant from school, more likely to be excluded from school, more likely to leave school at age 16, and less likely to attain academic and professional qualifications in adulthood." Theodore Dalrymple[36] expressed things more directly: "Britain's mass bastardy is not a sign of an increase in the authenticity of our human relations but a natural consequence of the unbridled hedonism that leads in short order to chaos and misery, especially among the poor."

We need Father Zeus to maintain order and stability therefore; not just to have power, but because without that maintenance, the alternative is not a 'better' world, a utopia, but increasing chaos, death and destruction. It is to move away from life – and the good life – and to return to the dog-eat-dog situation that Zeus surmounted.

In our next chapter we look at the Greek concept of hubris and how this is rampant in today's world in various ways.

---

[35] Source: Edward Kruk, Ph.D., "The Vital Importance of Paternal Presence in Children's Lives." May 23, 2012.
http://www.psychologytoday.com/blog/co-parenting-after-divorce/201205/father-absence-father-deficit-father-hunger
[36] Theodore Dalrymple, ibid.

Chapter 2:
Hubris and Apollo

The ancients really understood the psychology of the human mind; how it works and what it seeks; and most importantly what the consequences are for the hubris of ignoring the gods' advice or commands. Hubris, of course, for the Greeks was the ultimate sin, for it meant that one had either ignored or defied the express wishes of the gods. And we have to understand that although the gods – the Olympian gods that is – fought and bickered amongst themselves, had rivals and jealousies just like us, nevertheless the whole concept of them was that they had supplanted the chaos, primitivism and savagery of their fathers and mothers such as the Titans. They had replaced all that with order and justice. The world of Cronos (the father of Zeus), for example, seems bestial in comparison with the ordering of the cosmos his children created. Indeed, when we think of Cronos as a word for 'time', we know that time eats all her children, just as Cronos attempted to devour all his male off-spring.

Zeus changed all that – we now had order in the Cosmos; and more specifically in our world down below – beneath, in both senses of the word - Olympus, where gods resided. Hubris, then, was the worst possible sin. Peter Jones[37] describes it thus: "It [hubris] originally meant doing physical violence to someone; by extension, it came to mean humiliating someone in order to get the upper hand over them, to show them who was boss, physically or socially. The aim was to degrade or demean the other person, as Aristotle says, for the sheer pleasure of demonstrating your superiority. That was something no proud Greek would take from anyone; and no god would take from any mere mortal." Notice in this description of hubris there is an important sense of intention: one deliberately seeks others' harm and degradation; and as applied to humans and the gods, there is also a sense of defiance – 'demonstrating your superiority'.

If it isn't clear enough already, Stephen Kershaw expressed it pointedly thus: "Hubris is more than an attitude – it manifests itself in violent or arrogant actions (it was the Greek word for GBH)"[38.] Today – as a sidebar – whilst not always leading to GBH[39], we witness this sort of defiant attitude in schools with pupils' reaction and insolence to teachers with 'you can't touch me'; and with adults too we have the same sort of attitude to authorities and the police whereby people think they cannot be 'touched', which is

---

[37] Peter Jones, *Eureka! Everything you Wanted to know about the Ancient Greeks But were afraid to ask*
[38] *GBH: Grievous Bodily Harm*. From Stephen Kershaw, Classical Civilization, 2010.
[39] In the UK, GBH is a criminal offence and stands for Grievous Bodily Harm.

to be and to place oneself beyond law. Remember, not even Zeus was beyond the law!

There are so many examples of this hubris in the Greek myths, but perhaps my favourite of all is the one that Dante himself saw worthy of mention in his Inferno[40], Capaneus the Proud. The story, as told by Statius in his Thebaid, goes like this: Capaneus is one of the 7 heroes who have set out to destroy Thebes, and they assault the city. As a warrior, Capaneus is colossal, fearless and virtually unstoppable. He scales the walls on a ladder, and as he does so, screams out as he reaches the top[41] a taunt against all the gods in whom he does not believe:

> "Where are the sluggard sons of this accursed land, Bacchus and Alcides? Any lesser name I am ashamed to challenge. Rather come thou—what worthier antagonist? For lo! Semele's ashes and her tomb are in my power!—come thou, and strive with all thy flames against me, thou, Zeus! Or art thou braver at frightening timid maidens with thy thunder, and razing the towers of thy father-in-law Cadmus?"

Even the gods themselves, at this, began to wonder whether Zeus was able to stop the fearless Capaneus; but then:

> "Even as he spoke, the thunderbolt struck him, hurled with the whole might of Zeus: his crest first vanished into the clouds, the blackened shield-boss dripped, and all the hero's limbs were now illuminated. The armies both give way, in terror where he may fall, what squadrons he may strike with his burning body. He feels the flame hissing within him and his helmet and hair afire, and trying to push away the galling cuirass with his hand, touches the scorched steel beneath his breast. He stands nevertheless, and turning towards heaven pants out his life and leans his smoking breast on the hated battlements, lest he should fall; but his earthly frame deserts the hero, and his spirit is released; yet had his limbs been consumed a whit more slowly, he might have expected a second thunderbolt."

I quote the whole passage so that we can feel the total devastation from the god, Zeus: "helmet and hair afire," the "scorched steel," and even the sense of its decisive speed, for if it had taken a moment longer, Zeus would have sent a second bolt. Notice, too, the effect it has on all those around: both armies give way "in terror."

---

[40] Dante, *The Divine Comedy*, Inferno, Canto 14.
[41] Statius, Thebaid (10. 904-7).

Such, then, is the reward for hubris! Hubris leads to destruction. I quoted James Hollis[42] in the Introduction as noting that even the gods were subject to order, to justice, and that could mean Nemesis[43] or 'consequential retribution'. So here we see with Capaneus how his hubris leads to his nemesis; hubris is the cause of nemesis' effect. So, on a personal level it is important to live and walk humbly with our gods. Again, citing Hollis: "Jung disturbingly observed that what we have ignored or denied inwardly will then more likely come to us as outer fate." In other words, denial is a form of hubris which generates – and will generate - its own nemesis in our lives.

Indeed, it can be argued that denial is the very worst form of all psychological disturbances; keeping in mind, there are many other types of negative mindsets: control of reactions, repression, blame, identification, sublimation, withdrawal, projection, rationalization, and numbing; and all these strategies are defence mechanisms, designed to protect our own egos from being exposed (to some 'thing' that threatens or that it feels threatens its security or existence). But it would seem that denial is the worst of them and we see this in its most extreme form when the denial takes the specific form of 'denial of the truth'. From the Greek myth perspective, hubris is a form of denying the truth: the truth of who we are, and who we are in respect to the gods themselves.

'Denying the truth' is something today that seems to abound in our political, philosophical, educational, social and even scientific domains. A simple example would be the transgender issue in which it is seriously maintained that a man – XY chromosomes – can self-identify and be accepted as a 'real' woman. The sort of 'denying the truth' that is involved in these convoluted positions is nothing short of astonishing – and nothing short of hubris[44].

Before talking about hubris in more detail, let me reinforce that notion that denial is the worst of sins, not only from the Jungian perspective, the Greek hubristic perspective, and even the common-sense perspective of 'denying the truth' (seeming to be a pretty appalling state of mind), but it is also a deeply held Christian conviction too. For in Dante's Divine Comedy, Hell is full of those who have denied the truth: in Canto 3 of The Inferno[45] Virgil refers

---

[42] James Hollis, *Finding meaning in the second half of life*, 2006.
[43] Nemesis: represents retributive justice, often translated as "righteous indignation" or "revenge." Her role enforces balance by punishing hubris (excessive pride or arrogance) and ensuring that individuals do not overstep their rightful place. She restores equilibrium in cases where justice (Dike) has been violated.
[44] See Robert Oulds and Neil McCrae, *Moralitis, A Cultural Virus* 2020: 'As explained in a scathing critique by left-wing scientist Alan Sokal, post-modernism is damaging the very social justice causes that it was supposed to help, because it has abandoned reality in favour of an emotive and irrational phenomenology of grievance.'
[45] Dante, Inferno Canto 3. Lines 17-8, Peter Dale Translation.

to them in this way: it's a place where "you will see those wretched people lie / Who could the Good of Intellect dismiss." The intellect – which is good – is what we use to establish truth, to discover reality as it really is; and so to falsify it or ignore – to 'dismiss' - it for some other selfish end is a profound evil.

But we can take an earlier and greater authority than Dante's writing to validate this observation: Jesus Christ. In Mark, Luke and Matthew's gospel, Jesus warns against the sin of blasphemy against the Holy Spirit. What is this, but denial of what your own eyes have witnessed, as the text from Matthew[46] makes clear:

> "Therefore I tell you, every sin and blasphemy will be forgiven people, but the blasphemy against the Spirit will not be forgiven. And whoever speaks a word against the Son of Man will be forgiven, but whoever speaks against the Holy Spirit will not be forgiven, either in this age or in the age to come."

The context of this is that the Pharisees have seen the healing miracles of Christ, but have attributed them, not to the power of God, but to the power of devils and demons: flatly denying, in other words, what they had witnessed by equating a good act (healing) with evil. So, we see in Christianity too, there is this deep abhorrence of denial – in fact, it is a sin so deep that it cannot be forgiven, or so Christ asserts.

To return, then, to the Greek myths, one god in particular has much to say about hubris: the god Apollo. Apollo, Geri Giebel Chavis[47], tells us, is "patron god of music and poetry, is also recognized as the divinity of medicine and healing not only in his own right but also through his son, Aesculapius. Through the multifaceted Apollo, poetry is associated with light, sun, and prophecy." In short, Apollo is associated with order, form, creativity, beauty and, as the god of the sun, with light itself. As was pointed out in chapter 1, Apollo had three famous maxims, three principles of life by which to live by, and to transgress these three maxims was clearly to be hubristic. But before considering them, notice in passing the word 'transgress', since we shall be returning to it!

Apollo's three maxims were Know Thyself, Nothing in Excess and Surety Brings Ruin. Although an immortal god, Apollo's maxims sprang in some sense from his own experience; for, he overstepped the mark (more than once) and was punished for it by Zeus, his father.

---

[46] Matthew 12:31-32
[47] Poetry and Story Therapy, Geri Giebel Chavis, 2011

KNOW THYSELF

His maxim, Know Thyself, nowadays seems self-evidently clear; the whole Western personal development movement and its coaching methodologies in business and corporate life would appear to have acted on his advice in numerous ways including endless personality, psychometric, motivational maps, strengthsfinder and other diagnostics which are used to tell us exactly who we are (and tell our bosses and recruiters too)! This is good so far as it goes, but it is not the full meaning of what Apollo meant when he advised humans to know themselves. What he most profoundly meant was that human beings should not overstep the bounds of their humanity: they were not gods, and should not act as if they were. Such excessive pride and self-confidence (think Capaneus!) will lead to ruin. By knowing yourself, you were then able to acknowledge your limitations.

One of the most famous examples in the Twentieth Century of apparent hubris coming to ruin was the sinking of The RMS Titanic ship in 1912. The makers[48] of the ship did not claim the ship was 'unsinkable', but the media – based on its safety features – did; and the name the makers gave it, Titanic, referring to its seemingly unstoppable strength and power, alluded quite directly to the Titans of old that Zeus defeated: and sent to the Hell of Tartarus, deep beneath the surface of the Earth! Now The Titanic itself is in Tartarus, or more accurately about 2.37 miles underneath the ocean's surface with pressures of approximately around 380 times the atmospheric pressure at sea level! Wrecked then, and never to rise again – like the Titans.

One example in Apollo's own immortal life came when he, and his sister, Artemis (he the son and she the daughter of Zeus) took revenge on Zeus by killing the Cyclops, who were allies of Zeus and manufactured his famous thunderbolts. They did this because Zeus had struck dead (as we learnt earlier in Chapter 1) Aesculapius, the healer who raised the dead! Both Apollo, because Aesculapius was his son, and Artemis, because she'd asked Aesculapius to raise a dead friend of hers, Hippolytus, were upset with Zeus for this act. But as we explained before, raising the dead – a human to raise the dead – was against the divine order; indeed, Zeus saw it as a threat to that very order he had created. Apollo and Artemis, as his children, as the sun and moon respectively, were mediators of his own power and so expected to comply with the rules of the cosmos, as it were; but they didn't! They exceeded their limitations. So, as a punishment, Apollo, the great god of order, was forced to serve as a mortal man for a year in the court of a Greek king, Admetus.

---

[48] Harland and Wolff, Belfast.

It need hardly be said that today many human ambitions seem hubristic in exactly the way that Aesculapius's was: we want to live forever, we want to colonize Mars, and more mundanely, we want to end diseases, end war, end poverty, end inequality and any number of other things which are part of the human condition. One is not advocating a laissez-faire approach to life, or suggesting that things cannot be improved – as they certainly can and have (in some respects over the last two centuries) – but there is in almost all these utopian projects a sense of hubris: that through education, through 'progress', through human determination (without reference to the gods or God) that these goals are achievable.

Writing a century ago, GK Chesterton[49] said, "England has taken refuge in Utopia after Utopia of ever-mounting insanity, believing a world in which all labour and sorrow had vanished, with reforms by which every man could live to be three hundred years old ... And now, after a century of such nonsense, we stand where we did ..." Note, that was a century ago, and before science and technology had split the atom or sent men to the moon! But the desire for these reforms, and for these utopias seem even stronger than ever they were, back in GK Chesterton's days. As more recently, John Gray[50] writes: "... secular thinkers have turned to a belief in progress that is further removed from the basic facts of human life than any religious myth." The basic facts of human life, which are contained in the myths ... are being ignored or turned upside down.

NOTHING IN EXCESS

If we wish to live a good life, then, we must not imagine that we are gods and display this hubristic arrogance. And the second rule, Nothing in Excess, sometimes expressed as Not too Much, is similar; for it requires us as humans to have balance in everything. Balance and moderation were key to achieving a harmonious life and avoiding the destructive consequences of extremes. This principle applied to many areas, such as consumption, behaviour, ambition, and even virtues like courage or justice. The idea is to maintain equilibrium and avoid the pitfalls of excess, which could lead to downfall or suffering. In many respects it is equivalent to the Tao Te Ching and the Chinese view of yin and yang wherein the "the universe results from the constant and invisible harmonizing of its fundamental polarity, the yin-yang[51]." The word harmonizing here is important, for the good life is the harmonious life. In Eastern

---

[49] GK Chesterton, cited in *Wisdom and Innocence*, Joseph Pearce, 2015.
[50] John Gray, ibid.
[51] John Monbourquette, *How to Befriend your Shadow*, 2001.

thinking[52], "A controlled temperament bestows a sort of divine power."

Perhaps the most famous example in Greek myths of a mortal disobeying the injunction of Nothing in Excess was Midas, he of the golden touch! Midas committed a double hubris in fact: he had demanded an excessive gift from the god, Dionysus, and furthermore the gift itself threatened to destabilize the order of the cosmos, and so life itself. How could it not – his touch turning everything to gold? We remember that hubris in Greek thinking was the worst 'sin' of all. Asking for the ability to turning everything into gold was itself excessive – nothing balanced about that; and the gift was also arrogant and aggressive since it not only undermined the cosmos (imagine everything be turned to gold!) but gave him an unfair wealth advantage over all other human kings and mortal beings; it was inequitable too. We will look at this myth in a lot more detail in chapter 7.

But for now, two other myths are highly illustrative of the points I wish to make. First, the myth of Icarus. Icarus was the son of Daedalus, the great inventor. Daedalus crafted wings of feathers and wax so they could escape the labyrinth of Crete. Before taking flight, Daedalus warned Icarus not to fly too high, as the sun's heat would melt the wax. In his hubris, Icarus ignored his father's warning, delighting in the sensation of flight and soaring ever higher. As he approached the sun, the wax holding his wings together melted, and he plummeted into the sea, which now bears his name, the Icarian Sea. The arrogance of ignoring his father's wise advice here is shown most clearly in his ignoring the limits of what is possible for a human being; we said before that limitation was crucial.

The second myth connects us directly with Apollo who had so much to say about how to live your life well: the myth of Niobe. Niobe, a queen of Thebes, was blessed with many children— variously reported but usually given as 12 (the "Niobids"). At a ceremony in honour of Leto, goddess of motherhood, her maternal pride turned into hubris when she mocked the goddess Leto, who had had only two children (the twin deities Apollo and Artemis) and demanded that in future a cult should be set up in her own honour as she had six sons and six daughters, whereas Leto only had two. Thus, she claimed to be a superior mother and openly belittled Leto. Angered by her arrogance, Leto asks her children, Apollo and Artemis, to avenge this insult, which they willingly do: all of Niobe's children (or all but two, depending on the version) are killed. Niobe sees each of her children dying before her very eyes and in appalling agony. Devastated, Niobe fled to Mount Sipylus, where she was transformed – by Zeus - into a stone, and down from

---

[52] Donald G Krause, *The Way of the Leader*, 1997.

which her endless tears form a stream—a symbol of her eternal grief and the consequences of her hubris.

SURETY BRINGS RUIN

This final maxim of Apollo is more obscure than the other two, but it is equally pertinent and powerful. The phrase itself is often translated as 'Make a pledge and mischief is nigh,' or 'Give a pledge and trouble is at hand', which is perhaps the clearest statement of all. It's a warning against making rash promises or taking on obligations that one may not be able to fulfil. In ancient Greece, a pledge or guarantee (especially in financial or legal matters) could lead to significant trouble if things went wrong. The maxim encourages careful consideration before committing to anything, emphasizing the potential dangers of overconfidence and the importance of prudence and caution in decision-making.

An excellent example of the concept "Surety brings ruin" in Greek mythology is the story of Phaethon, the son of Helios (the Sun god). At this point, and before outlining the story, one should note a certain irony: the original god of the sun in Greek mythology was not Apollo, but Helios, a Titan. Eventually, Apollo displaced Helios as god of the sun, but with the blending of their mythologies over time, Phaethon came to be seen as Apollo's son; so, in one sense then, just as with Aesculapius being Apollo's son, Apollo is again at the centre of his own dictums.

The story runs that Phaethon was taunted by his peers who doubted his divine parentage from Helios/Apollo. Therefore, seeking proof of his lineage, Phaethon travelled to meet his father, and to reassure his son, Helios swore an unbreakable oath by the River Styx that he would grant Phaethon any wish as proof of his love and divinity. Remember what we said in Chapter 1 about oaths made by the River Styx: no god, including Zeus, could break them (without the whole Cosmos falling apart).

It was not enough, then, for his father to reassure him: he had to show off the fact. And so he asked for something incredibly dangerous: he wished to drive the chariot of the sun across the sky for a day, just as Helios did. Despite knowing and being warned of the dangers of this task, (his father begged him not to do it) —no mortal could control the fiery, powerful horses of the sun—Helios was bound by his oath and reluctantly allowed Phaethon to take the reins.

When Phaethon began his journey across the sky, his overconfidence and lack of skill quickly became apparent. The horses sensed that the driver was inexperienced and lost control. As the chariot veered off its course, the sun either came too close to the

Earth, scorching it, or went too far away, freezing it. This caused massive destruction and chaos in the world below.

Realizing the impending catastrophe, Zeus, intervened to prevent further ruin. He struck Phaethon down with a thunderbolt, killing him instantly and causing his body to fall into the river Eridanus. Phaethon's overconfidence—his surety—had led directly to his ruin, and by extension, brought havoc to the world.

The story of Phaethon embodies the idea that excessive confidence or recklessness—especially when taking on responsibilities beyond one's capability—can lead to disastrous consequences. Phaethon's fatal insistence on driving the chariot despite the warnings serves as a cautionary tale about the dangers of hubris and the peril of assuming certainty in an uncontrollable situation.

These maxims are deeply connected to the philosophical and ethical ideals of ancient Greece, particularly the emphasis on balance, self-knowledge, and wisdom. They reflect the Greeks' belief in the importance of living a life guided by reason, avoiding extremes, and understanding one's place in the cosmos: avoiding hubris! If you 'know yourself', if you practise 'nothing in excess', then you are less likely to be hubristic; finally, if you understand Surety Brings Ruin, then you begin to immunise yourself against hubris. What might this mean in practice?

Earlier I asked you to note the word 'transgress', and the adjective from it is 'transgressive'. Why? Because it is essentially the word and concept that most defines and even drives the kind of society we are currently living in. We talked of transgressing Apollo's three maxims, but as Theodore Dalrymple[53] observed, "To break a taboo or to transgress are terms of the highest praise in the vocabulary of modern critics, irrespective of what has been transgressed or what taboo broken." Everyone gets praised – adulated even – for 'breaking the rules.' This is an important point. It forms the basis of 'progressive' politics and also of modern and postmodern art, music, architecture, literature and thinking; and so naturally, it becomes the bedrock of our contemporary culture. So, the 'transgressive' generates the 'progressive', and the progressive has some 'utopia' as its end in sight.

To see what this means, consider this[54]: "Almost every major institution has DEI (diversity, equity and inclusion) departments, whose function is to make progressive ideas the norm. In fact, these ideas now constitute the state religion, and there are 'blasphemy laws' in place to protect it ... a defining characteristic of the elite is that it will never admit to being one."

---

[53] Theodore Dalrymple, *Our Culture, What's Left of It*, 2005
[54] Ed West, reviewing Matthew Goodwin, *Values, Voice and Virtue*, and cited in Money Week MW 21st April, 2023.

But as John Gray[55] noted, "Whatever role it may have had in the past, belief in progress has become a mechanism of self-deception that serves only to block perception of the evils that come with the growth of knowledge", and that would include self-knowledge (remember, know thyself?). To return to James Hollis' wisdom[56]: 'Utopian visions appear from time to time and never succeed in the test of real life, for they come from ego-driven 'good intentions' only, not the energies that give rise to the gods.'

There is, therefore, a sort of double fault going on: we practise hubris in the ways we have described by ignoring or disobeying Apollo's maxims, and we also fail to harness the energies of the gods – within us from a psychological perspective – and live on willpower and ego alone. Indeed, we thrust forward to be 'successful', to achieve and to dominate without any reference to the forces that we do not see, and which ultimately determine our destiny.

These forces we do not see act on us whether we are aware of them or not, and they are forces for order. The catastrophe of our time, therefore, results in another law being promulgated: the law of unintended consequences. As we run to achieve what we think we are achieving, we are in fact going to achieve exactly the reverse.

Before considering this on a large scale in chapter 3 when we think of hubris and the god Hermes, there is one more Greek myth that perfectly encapsulates the law of unintended consequences. This myth the greatest tragedians of ancient Greece tackled, and especially Sophocles in his Oedipus Rex: the story of King Oedipus.

Once more, Apollo is involved, since his prophecies were promulgated by the Oracle of Delphi and it was his prophecy before the birth of Oedipus that Oedipus would kill his father and marry his mother!! Both father, king Laius, and mother, queen Jocasta, attempted to thwart this prophecy: they could not murder their own son (that would have incurred the Furies' vengeance) but they left him to die, abandoned on a mountainside. This did not work; along the way in the story Oedipus himself got to learn the prophecy, and set out to make sure it could never come true. But inadvertently, he did kill his father without realising he had done so, and then – as a saviour (he outwitted and killed the Sphinx) – married his mother. The fact was that in solving the Sphinx' riddle, he clearly was the brightest and most able man of his time; but that was not enough to save him. Human intelligence is simply not enough to save us from the traps of time and the material world; everything he did to move away from fulfilling the prophecy, led him closer to completing it.

---

[55] John Gray, Heresies, 2004.
[56] James Hollis, ibid.

That is the situation that most people in the West are in now on a personal level: they want the good life, they want success, but in not submitting themselves to the Higher Power(s)[57], they are getting the reverse of what they actually want. We are addicted to our egos and cannot break the spell; only in submitting can we find true happiness. As Hollis[58] expressed it: "The traditional admonition to walk humbly and in fear of the gods has continuing meaning for us all."

---

[57] I use this expression advisedly because in Alcoholics Anonymous one of the key rules of the 12 rules of recovery is to submit to a higher power: https://www.alcoholics-anonymous.org.uk/about-aa/what-is-aa/12-steps/
[58] James Hollis, ibid.

Chapter 3:
Hubris and Hermes

In chapter 2 we considered the vice of hubris, very much from the perspective of the individual, and also with particular relevance to the 'offended' god, Apollo. I say offended because this is what the vices, especially hubris, does: it offends the gods, and as Jung[59] metaphorically expressed it: "a neurosis is an offended or neglected 'god'." So many of our psychological pathologies stem from this 'offending' of a god. And this is especially true when we start considering hubris not only on a personal level, but on a collective one too.

One god that stands out here is Hermes (frequently known in the West by his Latin name, Mercury). Hermes is the god that the modern Western world – and possibly all the world – now excessively worships, and it is the 'excessive', perhaps, wherein lies the offence. *The Penguin Book of Classical Myths*[60] describes him as 'a mobile divinity'! Consider his attributes: he is the god of 'ready speech' – of communications per se – and his winged cap, or petasos, signified he was a traveller (in other words, crossed boundaries or what in modern jargon is sometimes called 'liminal spaces'), his staff (in Latin, caduceus) indicated he was a herald (so a bearer of news), and his golden sandals had wings which meant he could fly across lands and seas with astonishing rapidity; the sandals also erased footprints, so nobody would know of his presence. What does this all sound like? The god of our modern world in which we can communicate with anyone, anywhere, anytime; we can have news 24/7 and break through even national boundaries and borders; and we can circle the world with instant communications. Plus, we can electronically cover our tracks in all sorts of ingenious ways.

And this last point leads on to the word itself: Hermes, from which we get phrases such as 'hermetically sealed', suggesting secrets that cannot be uncovered and discovered; and also, the word hermeneutics – meaning the art of interpretation of what is subtle, obscure, arcane and difficult.

All this sounds good and useful, but sadly there are two other sides to Hermes that we must draw into this discussion. First, that Hermes is often depicted as having a bag of money: he is the trickster god, the god of luck and the god of fraud, of merchants and of thieves. Moreover, of perjury too: the day he was born he stole Apollo's cattle and denied it to Apollo's face. Keep in mind, Apollo was not only a powerful god, but also his half-brother. It was only

---
[59] Cited in James Hollis, *Finding meaning in the second half of life*, 2006.
[60] Jenny March, *The Penguin Book of Classical Myths*, 2008.

when Apollo hauled him before Zeus, the king of the Gods, that Hermes was forced to confess his lies – even he dared not take on the lord of the universe, the king of all the gods.

This seems very relevant to the internet of things, the mobile devices, and the purposes to which we find they are being used. Increasingly, we are becoming aware of the frauds, thieves and general perjury ('fake news') that this communications revolution is promoting. As well, of course, as opening up some very deep and dark areas – gambling, pornography, terrorism and violence – even to children barely out of their diapers. This is Hermes in action. And here we might comment on the Roman name for the element we call mercury, quicksilver: for however useful it might be, silver is not gold; it is not the real, solid thing of value that gold is; it is a cunning counterfeit whose speed astonishes and attracts us. In the past we have taken it as medicine, especially for syphilis, but it is ultimately deadly and induces madness.

Which leads to the second side of Hermes: namely, his other title. He was known as 'psychopompos' because he was the guide of dead souls to Hades (the ultimate liminal space). Now we have to understand something very important to get the full picture of what this means. The kingdom of Hades – of Hell – was just as out of bounds to the other gods as Olympus was to Hades; for he himself never ventured to Olympus. Hades was a hateful place; the Greeks themselves detested it. Achilles was virtually inconsolable there when Odysseus met him on his 'living' trip into hell[61]. The gods on Olympus equally had a hatred and horror of the place and never went there. Why exchange their light and immortal ambrosia for the world of darkness and shadows?

Except, of course: Hermes was the one god permitted to visit Hades. He was the intermediary between the king of gods, Zeus, on Olympus, and the king of hell in Hades. He alone could navigate its dangers and illusions and madness – perhaps because he was as tricky as death itself and could not be caught or trapped there. But as Jung[62] wrote: "The journey to Hell means to become Hell itself". What this means is that the danger of worshipping Hermes potentially leads us – our souls – to Hell itself; only, unlike the god Hermes, once we are there, we invariably cannot come back.

This seems to me to be where the modern world is now: Hermes has not been offended or neglected, but on the contrary has been worshipped to such an extent that the human race is in danger of disappearing into an apocalyptic, technological hell which will make the bloodshed of the last century seem mild. For, how can it be that the last thing people now want to do at the point of death is

---

[61] Homer, the Odyssey, chapter 11. This is often called Nekyia, or "Book of the Dead."
[62] James Hollis, ibid.

not to pray but to check their mobiles one more time?

So, on the one hand we have a god who is over-worshipped, if I may be permitted to express it that way; and on the other, if that is the case, there must be a god who is neglected – aside that is, from all the other 12 on Olympus? And perhaps it is no surprise if I say that this god is Apollo, the half-brother and best friend of Hermes! On day one of his life, Hermes killed a tortoise and from its shell made the first lyre. When he played it, he mesmerised Apollo; and then gave the lyre as a gift to Apollo; ever after Apollo became the god of music and poetry. And so, Apollo forgave Hermes for stealing his cattle and they became best friends. But notice the link: the god of communication makes the technology that generates the music; indeed, which makes 'art'. Apollo is the god of light, reason, proportion, poetry and healing. This is the god that we have neglected and offended (as we saw in chapter 2); and as the worship of Hermes (and technology) has increased, our art is not art, our music is not music, and our poetry is lacking form, meter, rhyme and more generally speaking, beauty, and so is in short mostly drivel; no wonder there is little healing in the world – because technology has taken over, has swamped the creativity that humans have naturally got with its ersatz substitutions. We have to return to the god Apollo in our subconscious minds if we are to rescue ourselves from the technological madness that the idolatry of Hermes has created. This is the challenge for our age now.

It should be clear from what I have said so far that this excessive Hermes' induced hubris is as much about collective madness as it is personal; this is because of the very nature of the 'hermetic' technology itself. Yes, someone on their deathbed may well be wishing to check their mobile phone one more time; and yes, aren't we just sick of seeing even lovers in restaurants, sitting facing each other and waiting for the food to arrive, and whilst they do, not whispering sweet nothings to each other as lovers were wont to, but each tapping madly into their own mobile; and yes, haven't we seen mothers and fathers with babies, children, and pets in the park making calls, oblivious to the company they are with? Yes, this is all personal and so works at the individual level; but Hermes' worship is also collective too.

Let's consider three areas in the last few years where we have had amazing, mind-boggling concepts from the super-rich and super-powerful elites who, though unelected, seem to have extraordinary influence over governments, academic institutions and the working lives of ordinary people – and who worship Hermes!

In no particular order these three ideas are: one, from Elon Musk[63,] that we can go to Mars and live there. This is only possible, of course, because of the science and technology; but consider the vaulting ambition involved, not only in constructing the technology to transport us, but in the idea that we can, as humans, live in the 'heavens', as it were; that we can actually conquer the heavens – other worlds – and make them our own. Plus, combine this with the notion that Earth itself is not sufficient – how disrespectful might that seem to the gods? Why are we not making life on Earth better now, rather than taking a shot – a very long shot – at some future life elsewhere? The worship of Hermes goes along with that human tendency to create utopias.

Second, we find that someone – some 'ones' – think it a good idea for NASA[64] to spend $324.5M to propel a rocket into space in order to save the world! This saving the world involves crashing into an asteroid to alter its orbit. Does this not remind us of Oedipus, whom we met at the end of chapter 2, who learned from a prophecy that he would kill his father and marry his mother fled Corinth, and by fleeing thereby managed to unintentionally fulfil the prophecy. Do we really know enough to know what will happen if we change the course of an asteroid? If we could actually accurately predict next week's weather I might have more confidence in this hubristic activity, but since we can't even predict that with any certainty, then one is fearful of the consequences of such dramatic actions. The Law of Unintended Consequences is another way of expressing what I am contending is actually the wrath of the gods, or their sense of irony.

Third, and perhaps most worrying of all, we have the irrepressible Bill Gates and his Sun-dimming technology[65]? What is this? Well, we are intent on blocking sunshine in order to prevent global warming? Aside from all the other factors involved in climate change, one striking thing we learn from Jeremy Nieboer[66] is this astonishing piece of research: "On a global scale an analysis of 75,225,200 deaths in 13 countries over the period 1985-2012 with wide ranges of climate conditions revealed that cold weather kills 20 times more than hot weather." Before commenting, I think we would all agree that research involving 75M+ people is large scale research! I would hazard a guess, then, that blocking the sun is going to make 'things' colder! What strikes one, yet again, is the hubris of these actions – taken without reference to ordinary

---

[63] https://www.youtube.com/watch?v=GZ1cyRCUBP4 When I wrote this, Donald had not yet been re-elected President of the USA and Elon Musk had not yet been appointed to a senior position in his government; this fact makes no difference to the thrust of my argument.
[64] https://www.theepochtimes.com/nasa-holds-press-briefing-on-planetary-defense-test_4746163.html
[65] https://www.forbes.com/sites/arielcohen/2021/01/11/bill-gates-backed-climate-solution-gains-traction-but-concerns-linger/
[66] Jeremy Nieboer, *Climate: All is Well, All Will be Well*, 2021.

people, local communities, and in flat defiance of the gods and the limitations of being human.

I am not a scientist, and neither am I pretending to be one, but I do think any rational mind can see the overreach implicit – if not explicit – in these human endeavours, however much they may be well-intentioned (or not). The equivalent Biblical story that expresses this level of hubris is the building of the Tower of Babel[67]: this too was a technological achievement (or would have been if it had succeeded) and its purpose was to reach heaven, and for us, therefore, to be gods. It came collapsing down, as God Himself intervened; how did God specifically intervene? If we consider it in terms of Greek mythology, the confusion of the languages of the world is tantamount to saying that Hermes was shut down! And similarly, in Greek myths, we find that Nemesis intervenes however powerful Hermes may think he is. Without, therefore, wishing to sound pessimistic, we can expect these grandiose plans – like the Tower of Babel - to fail, and disastrously so.

If we dig a little more deeply into this, we can go back to The Enlightenment of the Eighteenth century. The 'Thinkers' of the Enlightenment (note that word 'light' contained in the word 'Enlight-enment', and note too that the Titan Prometheus' hubris[68] was to steal fire for man – fire producing light) who, according to the philosopher John Gray. "...saw themselves as reviving paganism, but they lacked the pagan sense of the dangers of hubris. With few exceptions, these savants were actually neo-Christians, missionaries of a new gospel more fantastical than anything in the creed they imagined they had abandoned." This new gospel, of course, replacing Christianity and all organised religions, was the gospel[69] of 'reason'; that through reasoning human beings could create a utopia on Earth and be free of God - and the gods - once and for all.

Thus, the god Hermes is entirely implicated in The Enlightenment and its utopian plans for humanity. By now you are probably wondering, since I have mentioned 'utopian' or 'utopia' a couple of times, what I mean by this, or is it simply a case of the three pathologies I have outlined above? No, it is not just those three pathologies; it goes much deeper.

In the first instance, we need to understand what the word 'utopia' means etymologically, where does it come from? The word

---

[67] Genesis, chapter 11. 1-9.
[68] The word Prometheus means 'forethought' and although he was a Titan, he was not cast down to Tartaros with most of his brethren because – having foresight – he saw Zeus would win and sided with him. He knew, too, that in helping man with fire, he would suffer a terrible punishment from Zeus.
[69] Norman Doidge in Foreword to Jordan B Peterson's 12 Rules for Life, 2018: "Communism borrowed from the story of the Children of Israel in Egypt, with an enslaved class, rich persecutors, a leader, like Lenin, who goes abroad, lives among the enslavers, and then leads the enslaved to the promised land (the utopia; the dictatorship of the proletariat)."

first appeared in 1516 in the work (written in Latin) called Utopia by Sir Thomas More, an English statesman and philosopher. It comes from the Greek language: "ou-topos," meaning "no place" or "nowhere," and "eu-topos," meaning "good place." In other words, there is a dual meaning—something that is both an ideal place and a place that does not exist—which captures the essence of a concept that is both idealistic but more probably satiric: such a place could not and cannot be found!

More conceived of Utopia as an island society where all property is communal, people work for the common good, and there is religious tolerance and rational governance. The residents live according to reason and justice, leading lives that are free from the corruption, poverty, and inequality that plagued Europe at the time. And – which plague us now. Hence, the forever-hunger for a utopia where these problems do not exist. But what does this account of utopia sound like – 'property is communal, people work for the common good'[70]? Yes, you've guessed it: Communism, which still exists …nowhere! Since when or where has it ever worked?

Enlightenment: reason; Utopia: Communism – surely these are good things? Within measure, they might be, but that is not how history has played out. As reason – or perhaps Reason – has unfolded itself in Western historical fact, the god Hermes's role was central: as the communicator, as the technological innovator, as the crosser of boundaries, and as the fraudster, the West was sold a pup, which in the imaginative world of literature is best described as a Frankenstein[71] – a monster who should be dead but is made to come alive, and repeatedly, time and time again. As Hollis[72] correctly observed: "Our hubristic belief that we are in control of ourselves and nature only makes us more unconscious of what is at work within us."

This blindness to the forces unconsciously at work within us – for all the so-called 'reason' that was being practised – led to World Wars 1 and 2, where the god Ares[73] was present for sure, but it was the nature of the technology that turned these wars into such killing-fests and whose potential for more of the same is still with us today. At the same time as these events were developing, society was reaching out for an alternative Utopia. This manifested itself as

---

[70] Writing quite recently in Money Week, Stuart Watkins notes: "The idea of a universal basic income … Thomas More was one of the first to propose something like it in his Utopia in the C16th." MW 27/3/2020.
[71] Mary Shelley, Frankenstein, 1818. The sub-title of the work was, The Modern Prometheus, which directly links it to the mythologies we are discussing.
[72] James Hollis, ibid.
[73] Ares, called Mars by the Romans, was the god of war.

Communism[74]. For, as Karl Popper[75] observed: "Those who promise us paradise on earth never produced anything but hell."

Now it may seem a stretch suggesting our two World Wars were caused by the simple act of worshipping 'reason' (for that in effect is what the Enlightenment initiated, and what has been going on ever since[76]) and that the god, Hermes, was instrumental in 'making them happen'; but it would also not only be a 'stretch' but also a profound irony of the unintentional, Oedipus type: for the fanatics of this creed also and specifically sought to destroy Christianity and religions more generally, which they perceived as superstitions, and replace them with 'reason'. But not just superstitions: religions they also held responsible for wars, crusades, inquisitions and the evils of the world. If only one could be rid of religion, and replace it with reason, then the world would be a better place by far – utopia would be just round the corner in fact.

The thing is, though, in destroying religions, superstitions and mythologies (including viewing Greek myths as no more than harmless, pointless, irrelevant fairy stories) something else gets destroyed in the process, something invaluable, and something which for all his power, Hermes does not represent in any meaningful way: namely, morality. By morality I mean the distinction between right and wrong, between evil and good. You will remember that two of the first things that Hermes did on the initial day of his immortal life were to: steal Apollo's cattle, and then to lie to him. Apollo, the god of reason and clarity though, was not so easily fooled, and Hermes was called to account; nevertheless, if he can, he will defraud you!

We need to be clear here about morality. GK Chesterton[77] perceptively remarked that, "Morality did not begin by one man saying to another, 'I will not hit you if you do not hit me'; there is no trace of such a transaction. There is a trace of both men having said, 'We must not hit each other in the holy place'. They gained their morality by guarding their religion." One implication of this is that morality is not transactional – it requires a transcendental source, which there is some innate human recognition of in all serious religions. To do away with them then, the question becomes: how do we establish morality?

To establish morality is of vital importance because "Morality is not one sub-system among others, such as that there is

---

[74] Communism itself, Or Marxism, are all is manifestations of scientific materialism and in their own way are all ersatz religions.
[75] Karl R. Popper, *The Open Society and its Enemies*, 1945.
[76] We see this today in the status and seemingly unquestionable authority accorded to science and scientific 'experts' – the Covid epidemic and the response of 'science' to it was chilling in most countries. Perhaps Sweden alone as a whole country actually followed the 'science'.
[77] GK Chesterton, Orthodoxy, 1908

art, science, religion, business, politics, and so forth, alongside morality. Instead, morality is the guiding principle for all human endeavors[78]." We cannot do without morality, and without the 'holy place', transcendental source, we are left – as the French Revolutionaries were, as the Soviet master planners were, as Pol Pot was – to invent morality for ourselves: indeed, as George Orwell described it in his novel, 1984, the beginning of the creation of a new morality is the redefinition of the old words or terminologies. In other words, recasting language: speech – Hermes' domain - becomes tricky and treacherous.

Indeed, the centrality of morality in our lives simply cannot be overstated; neither can the importance of its derivation from a transcendental source, for without that source, morality becomes merely a matter of personal opinion. As it says in the Bible[79], "In those days there was no king in Israel; everyone did what was right in his own eyes." The result: total chaos, mayhem and a breakdown of society verging on anarchy.

Socrates, in various works[80], is attributed with thinking that two key ideas suggested the existence of a transcendent reality: the stars above (the design of the Cosmos: what we see externally) and the moral law within (what we know internally). These, if you will, constituted a kind of 'proof' (though not like 'proofs' of subsequent Christian apologists such as Anselm and Aquinas). In Plato's Apology, and the account of Socrates' defence during his trial, Socrates claims to follow a divine mission or inner "daimonion" (a divine voice or what we might call a conscience) that guides him toward virtuous actions. He suggests that his sense of morality and duty is rooted in something beyond human society, implying the existence of transcendental – divine - authority over moral truths and from which they derive.

In terms of the West's modern obsession with well-being, this morality issue is crucial from the Greek perspective, not only via their myths but also via their philosophies. As Neel Burton[81] puts it: "Socrates argues that justice and injustice are to the soul as health and disease are to the body: if health in the body is intrinsically desirable, then so too is justice in the soul." Well-being is intimately connected to morality in other words. And taking this a step further in order to be explicit, "… the aim of human life, and hence of social life, is not freedom but virtue."[82]

How far is this from today's thinking where not even freedom (or the old word, liberty) is generally considered to be the

---

[78] Mark William Roche, Why Literature Matters, 2004.
[79] Judges 21:25 (NASB)
[80] Plato's Phaedo, Timaeus, and for the moral argument, Euthyphro, Apology and Republic.
[81] Neel Burton, The Meaning of Myth.
[82] Leo Strauss, cited Grant Havers, Historical Revisionism on the Right, Chronicles, March 2020.

raison d'etre of society, and of each individual? Instead, what we have as the most common position: everyone wants to be, and expects to be allowed to be, 'happy'[83]. There is, of course, no god of 'happy'[84]! Happiness tends to be a by-product of engagement in something else: "I cannot believe that the purpose of life is to be happy. I think the purpose of life is to be useful, to be responsible, to be compassionate. It is, above all, to matter, to count, to stand for something, to have made some difference that you lived at all."[85] We may disagree with the items in the foregoing list, but certainly cannot doubt that seeking to be happy is not the aim; and happiness, too, must not be confused with achieving peace of mind.

Another view on this from the organisational cultural perspective is: "One misconception about highly successful cultures is that they are happy, light-hearted places. This is mostly not the case. They are energised and engaged, but at their core, their members are orientated less around achieving happiness than around solving hard problems together."[86] In short, the idea that we can all be 'happy' is not only another form of utopian thinking, but it is also a delusional, will o' the wisp pursuit that does not lead to happiness, because it must fail. Again, remembering Hollis[87], "Utopian visions appear from time to time and never succeed in the test of real life, for they come from ego-driven 'good intentions' only, not the energies that give rise to the gods."

Thus, we come full circle to the 'energies that give rise to the gods' – these are the only energies that can lead us to success, or – to use another Greek myth – get us home to Ithaca and Penelope, as Odysseus got home, just (see chapters 11 and 12 for much more on Odysseus)! I say 'just' because he did upset - almost fatally – the god of the sea, Poseidon. But fortunately for him, he loved the goddess, Pallas Athene, and she loved him. This goddess of wisdom steered him through all his travails. And where was home, Ithaca? And who was his wife, Penelope? Was she in fact the finding – or re-uniting – with his own soul? Our next chapter investigates this most powerful god, Athene.

---

[83] A good overview of this phenomenon as big business is to be found in William Davies, The Happiness Industry, 2015.
[84] An interesting sidebar on this is: "A person cannot tell whether they were truly happy until they die; happiness is a reflection of the shape of a life as a whole, not a measure of isolated or even extended moments in it" - Mark Vernon, How to be an Agnostic, 2011
[85] Leo Rosten, Passions & Prejudices: Or, Some of My Best Friends are People, 1978
[86] Daniel Coyle, *The Culture Code*, 2019.
[87] Hollis, ibid.

Chapter 4:
Wisdom and Athene

In today's Western world, the focus has shifted away from salvation and the spiritual rewards of religion to personal development and self-actualization. This mindset permeates our culture in countless ways. One of its key messages is linked to the popular saying, "you only live once," encouraging people to make the most of life and "fulfil" themselves in the present. The implicit command is to squeeze every drop of experience from life, ensuring nothing is missed before it ends. This is why "bucket lists" have become so popular—it's almost seen as a moral failing, if not a social misstep, not to complete everything on your list. There's an urgency to stay busy. And adding to this drive, perhaps the most common parental goal for children today is their "happiness"—happiness has become the ultimate purpose of life as we noted in the previous chapter.

Moreover, this self-actualization is all about perfecting the "self," a term that has replaced the older concept of the "soul." While they might overlap in some contexts, their meanings are diverging. The ancient notion of the soul referred to the immaterial, immortal essence of a person—something deeply valuable, yet flawed, requiring "saving," whether through God or through practices like Buddhism's Eightfold Path. In fact, all religions exist because humans recognize their imperfection and sense that they need something greater than themselves to achieve salvation. Religions offer steps or practices to free us from cycles of sin or desire.

Self, on the other hand, is ... 'Me': a good person who needs to do more yoga, be vegan, 'be kind', in order to 'realize' that perfection that is already there, already in me. Hence, all the lessons on-line showing us how to defeat 'imposter syndrome'. The key mantra here is that we need to tell ourselves, 'I am good enough'. In a weird way, I don't need to do anything at all (so forget the yoga, veganism and kindness): I just have to believe in 'myself' and my true amazing 'perfections' will shine forth and I will never be an imposter again!

Of course, the idea that "you only live once" isn't a factual statement but rather a risky assumption. As Peter Stanford[88] pointed out, "We imagine we are so much more intelligent than past generations, believing that their wisdom can be surpassed by our own, filtered through science, logic, and reason. This leads to misleading and disheartening results." Roger Scruton[89] echoed this sentiment, observing: "A strange superstition has arisen in the

---

[88] Peter Stanford, Heaven, 2002.
[89] Roger Scruton, "Becoming a Family," Spring 2001 issue of City Journal: https://www.city-journal.org/article/becoming-a-family?utm_source=chatgpt.com

Western world that we can start everything anew, remaking human nature, society, and happiness, as though the knowledge and experience of our ancestors no longer mattered."

Perhaps the real truth is that we live twice. Nearly all ancient cultures believed this, and today, the majority of people do too— around 84% of the global population holds some form of religious belief[90]. This is why Pascal's Wager remains such a compelling argument. In simple terms, the wager suggests that it is rational to believe in God. If you believe and God exists, the reward is immense. However, if you don't believe and God does exist, the consequences could be severe. If God doesn't exist, both believers and non-believers face the same outcome: oblivion. Therefore, the argument favours belief in God, implying that life doesn't end with death but continues—so, in a sense, we live not just once, but twice.

Pascal also made the point that it was not only a question of whether God did or did not exist in terms of heaven and hell; he argued that there were moral benefits in believing in God. Having mentioned, then, Buddhism and the Eightfold Path (and even though Buddhism is not a theistic religion), nevertheless, it too has a moral dimension: to accept Buddhism is to accept the validity of the Eightfold Path, and this path, like the Ten Commandments, enjoins one to act morally.

And, interestingly, enough, it is the moral question that virtually dominates the ancient world and its view of the afterlife. By moral I mean: what is right and what is wrong? This means asking: have we lived in accordance with the deepest precepts of our society's values as well as our own consciences? As the great Roman writer Cicero[91] put it, "Away, then, with sharp practice and trickery, which desires, of course, to pass for wisdom, but is far from it and totally unlike it. For the function of wisdom is to discriminate between good and evil; whereas, inasmuch as all things morally wrong are evil, trickery prefers the evil to the good."

So, we come to the key word: 'wisdom'. Wisdom is what we have when we can distinguish between good and evil, and this constitutes the basis for a true morality. When we think about it, it is the moral question – what is right and what is wrong? – that dominates every aspect of our society now, not just in the past. As Aristotle[92] expressed it, "Every art and every inquiry, and similarly every action and pursuit, is thought to aim at some good; and for this reason, the good has rightly been declared to be that at which

---

[90] According to a 2012 study by the Pew Research Center, approximately 84% of the global population was affiliated with a religion: https://www.pewresearch.org/religion/2012/12/18/global-religious-landscape-exec/?utm_source=chatgpt.com More recent data from 2022 suggests some 85.8% have religious beliefs.
[91] Marcus Tullius Cicero, De Officiis (On Duties), specifically Book III, section 71.
[92] Aristotle, Nicomachean Ethics (Book I, Chapter 1).

all things aim." So, it follows that if morality is the key issue for us all, then acquiring wisdom must be the natural consequence of this. In Biblical terms[93] this is expressed as: "The fear of the Lord is the beginning of wisdom, And the knowledge of the Holy One is understanding."

To pursue wisdom, then, is a spiritual undertaking rather than a secular one. The Greeks knew this very well, which is why they had a god of wisdom, or more accurately, a goddess: Pallas Athene. And she, interestingly, was the favourite offspring of her father, the supreme god, Zeus. In a way, without making too much of the parallel, this echoes the account in the book of Proverbs of the relationship between the creation of the world by God and the personification, [94]Wisdom. Wisdom and the supreme Power (God), in other words, are locked in some intimate, unbreakable and inconceivable relationship that we can only approach figuratively. Christianity would go on to develop this relationship into the doctrine of the Trinity. But what can we learn from Greek mythology about wisdom and its goddess? Are there aspects of her being that are relevant and/or insightful for our lives today?

So, how did wisdom come about in Greek thinking? The origins - never mind the subsequent deeds of Athene - are fascinating in themselves, and possibly most instructive of all. We recall that 'father' Zeus had become king of the gods, and supreme ruler of the cosmos. This had come about because – in brief – Uranus the original sky god had been dethroned by his son, the Titan, Cronos, who in turn was dethroned by his son, Zeus. However, we need to be clear that this was not just a changing of the guard: it involved a fundamental shift in the nature of the universe. The Titans, of which Cronos was the king, were primeval and chaotic beings; what Zeus and the Olympians brought to the cosmos was rule, order, justice: they completely redefined and reformed what the cosmos was and is.

We could speculate, in an evolutionary sense, that the universe's development mirrors a process of chaos and transformation—massive movements of gas, explosions, black holes, and more. Yet, from this chaos emerges order, organization, and eventually life. In the early stages, represented by Uranus and his son Cronus, there is no sense of conscious thought or planning; they simply act and react. But with the arrival of Zeus, we see the emergence of a mind capable of understanding, ruling, and

---

[93] Proverbs 9.10

[94] Both 'chokhmah' in Hebrew and 'sophia' in Greek are feminine nouns in their respective languages, though Christians usually consider Wisdom to be the pre-incarnate Christ: The Word that was made flesh. Just as in the Greek myth, Athene is the favourite of the supreme, father god, so in Proverbs (chapter 8), "Wisdom ... I was constantly at his side. I was filled with delight day after day, rejoicing always in his presence, rejoicing in his whole world and delighting in mankind."

maintaining order. Zeus's role includes defeating evil, as seen when he conquers the dragon Typhon.

At this critical point, Zeus, although preparing to marry Hera, queen of the gods, is also involved with Metis, the Titaness whose name means "cunning intelligence" or "wisdom." They love each other, but both are cautious. Zeus is aware of a prophecy that Metis's child will surpass its father in greatness. To prevent this, Zeus tricks Metis into transforming into a fly while he becomes a lizard, and he promptly swallows her. With that, Zeus believes he has eliminated the threat of a more powerful offspring. However, the cunning of Metis proves stronger than Zeus's trickery.

Rather than a typical union, Metis has achieved what she intended: instead of a sexual relationship, she has merged entirely with Zeus by being ingested. Zeus, now confident that Metis poses no further threat, returns to his wedding celebrations. But later, he begins to suffer from a terrible headache that becomes so intense it nearly destroys him. The king of the gods is in agony, and no one can help—until Prometheus advises Hephaestus on what to do.

At this point, it's important to recognize the symbolic meaning of each character. Prometheus, a Titan who sided with Zeus against his fellow Titans, acts out of foresight—his name means "forethought." He wisely predicted that Cronos would lose to his son, Zeus, and chose to ally with the victors. Forethought, like cunning, is a form of wisdom. Meanwhile, Hephaestus, known by his Roman name Vulcan, is the god of metalwork and the son of Zeus and Hera. Though lame, Hephaestus is a master craftsman who forges weapons for the gods, symbolizing his role as their protector.

Keeping these two points in mind, then, Prometheus instructs Hephaestus to go get his axe and what to do with it. Zeus is persuaded into having his head split in two by the axe of Hephaestus! (One could speculate here on the right and left sides of the frontal cortex being divided[95], but that is too much of a distraction!). All the gods witness this: horrified at first as the skull splits open, and then utterly amazed, as from the breach in the head, a spear point first appears, followed by - fully-armoured - the goddess Athene.

Here is another parallel between the Greek myth of wisdom and wisdom in the Bible. Wisdom is not born through the flesh, through sex and biology, it is born parthenogenetically, which means in common discourse: a virgin birth. And the extraordinary thing to note about this immediately, is that wisdom is sui generis – and one of its attributes is that it is fully armed. It does not need to arm itself, prepare itself, for in its essential nature it is armed.

---

[95] For more on this, Iain McGilchrist, The Master and his Emissary, 2009.

It comes fully-bodied in herself – fully sufficient, fully able, fully powerful. And again, to refer back to the Bible, one little noted aspect of the life of Jesus is this: he is constantly under verbal attack and challenge, but there is not one recorded instance where he is at a loss for an effective and decisive response. Where did this man get his education, the Pharisees and teachers bewail? Who 'taught' him? He is not 'educated', so how can he answer in these ways? But what the myth is telling us is that education is not the same as wisdom, and may well be at variance with it[96].

Indeed, it is telling us that wisdom has an axiomatic power; it is foundational – it precedes what we might term 'thinking about' things. In other words, there is something intuitive about it: it rises from the depths of our psyches, as it were. And we all know this to be true when we witness ordinary people exhibiting more 'wisdom', or sometimes we might call it common sense, than the 'wise' of our age.

An example that strikes one immediately to illustrate this point is the various and recent university testimonies before the American Congress. Here we have the intellectual elite – the 'wise' of this world - coming up short in the context of real wisdom – which is to distinguish between the good and the bad. Especially egregious was the testimony of Professor Claudine Gay, who subsequently had to resign as President of Harvard. Of her, Republican congresswoman Elise Stefanik[97] said: "Her answers were absolutely pathetic and devoid of the moral leadership and academic integrity required of the president of Harvard". How can it be that someone so 'educated', could be so lacking in wisdom? Sadly, perhaps, because today education has been divorced from wisdom – and its goddess!

And this leads to one final point about the virgin birth of Athene: that is, one of the first things Athene does on being 'born' is request from her father, Zeus, that she ever remains a virgin! Which he grants. What this means, of course, is that wisdom is pure, unsullied, uncorrupted by carnality; further, it maintains an independence or objectivity of viewpoint, because it is not contaminated by 'relationships' or even one special relationship that might cause bias or partiality. She is the Eternal Virgin who cannot be defiled. The idea that knowledge is objective, and that subjectivity itself is subject to 'reality' is an antidote to so much contemporary thinking.

For those who think this is all 'pagan' and purely a Greek phenomenon (as opposed to a profound psychological and spiritual

---

[96] Roger Scruton alludes to just this point when he says, "After all, it needs a lot of education to realize that education is not so very important"– Roger Scruton, In Loco Parentis, Against the Tide, 2022.

[97] https://stefanik.house.gov/2024/1/statement-on-long-overdue-resignation-of-harvard-president?utm_source=chatgpt.com

insight common to all humanity), it is interesting to compare what the apocryphal book of The Wisdom of Solomon[98] says about wisdom; the parallels are striking: "There is in her [Wisdom] a spirit that is intelligent, holy, unique, manifold, subtle, mobile, clear, unpolluted, distinct, invulnerable, loving the good, keen, irresistible, beneficent, humane, steadfast, sure, free from anxiety, all-powerful, overseeing all, and penetrating through all spirits that are intelligent, pure, and altogether subtle. For wisdom is more mobile than any motion; because of her pureness she pervades and penetrates all things. For she is the breath of the power of God, and a pure emanation of the glory of the Almighty; therefore, nothing defiled gains entrance into her. For she is a reflection of eternal light, a spotless mirror of the working of God, and an image of his goodness.". This language gives a grander flavour to the nature of the goddess we are dealing with.

Let's now consider the acts of the goddess Athene and how they apply to us. She is the goddess of wisdom, and in that sense is the extension of her father, Zeus, the supreme god, whose victory ended the chaos and destructive powers of the cosmos up to that point after its creation. The first thing, then, to notice about Athene is her appearance. Three points here are of particular importance: she carried a spear, she held a shield, and she wore an aegis (which is thought to be a goatskin covering).

In reverse order: the aegis is protection. Even today we speak of someone who is 'under the aegis of', meaning the protection of, and the authority of, someone or something else. Wisdom is a high authority and source of protection. The shield she carries has emblazoned on its front the head of Medusa: it is literally 'petrifying', turning to stone whoever looks upon it. Metaphorically, the shield isn't just a protection, but a form of offence: it terrifies its enemies. Indeed, even today those who speak wisdom or what is sometimes called 'truth to power' are terrifying to their enemies, who simply cannot abide the truth. Finally, her spear represented her wisdom in strategic warfare and her upholding of justice, punishing evil-doers, especially those guilty of hubris; it was the sharp point of her power.

She was the goddess of wisdom, so how did this specifically manifest itself in her actions? Two areas here are really interesting. First, she was quite specifically a benefactor of humanity. She invented, inter alia, the trumpet, the flute, the earthenware pot, the plough, the rake, the ox-yoke, the horse bridle, the chariot, and the ship; it was she who first taught the science of numbers, cooking, weaving, and spinning. All very useful, and all very cultivated and cultivating - we are getting, via Athene, to what we might call civilisation.

---

[98] New Revised Standard Version, chapter 7, verses 22-26

That leads to the specific example of the Athenians wanting to name their city: was it to be named after the god Poseidon (a very powerful god and brother of Zeus) or after Athene? In the contest that ensued, Poseidon demonstrated his power by producing a saltwater spring, which was nice but of what use? Whereas Athene produced for them an olive tree, leading to fruit, oil and wood! Hence, and ever since, we have the city named as Athens in her honour – perhaps the most famous city in the world for its philosophers and much else besides that has determined Western culture.

If this all, in itself, were not enough to demonstrate the power of wisdom and the 'wisdom of following wisdom', then the second area of her excellence is even more striking. She is the great encourager of the Greek heroes. Professor Peter Levi[99] described her as the 'nurse of all heroes'. This is hardly surprising, given her excellence in strategic warfare. But before considering examples of this, and to avoid confusion: Ares (called Mars in the Latin tongue) is also the Greek god of war; but war here means the actual fighting, the blood and guts of war, the getting into the action type of war. Athene is the goddess of strategic warfare – the planning, the stratagems, the ruses that lead to victory. When Ares and Athene worked together, they were unstoppable; but when they were opposed, Athene always won – the Trojan War being a classic example, since they were on opposite sides. Brute strength is not enough to win – ask many of the opponents of Muhammed Ali in the ring: many were stronger than Ali, but the goddess of 'ring strategy' was his frequent saviour!

This encouragement of the Greek heroes really is part of the mandate to create a world of peace and order. Aside from the Titans, some even of the gods were disorderly, most famously Dionysus; but 'Athene did not permit his goat in her terrain.' So, it is Athene who watches over Heracles, who cleanses the world (imperfectly, admittedly) from terrors, monsters and injustice; it is Athene who supports Perseus in his quest against Medusa; it is Athene who helps construct the ship Argo, on which Jason and the Argonauts sail; and it is Athene who helps Theseus in his adventure against the Minotaur. It is worth noting on this last point that not only was she helping Theseus (an Athenian appropriately) defeat a monster, but also a monstrous injustice – the blood sacrifice of innocents at an annual event.

But perhaps the most well-known and extraordinary encouragement of heroes comes at the very end of the Greek hero line: we move from the golden age of heroes, Herakles, to the silver age of Theseus, to the bronze and last age of the real heroes, Achilles, who was half-immortal. However, in the final Trojan War

---

[99] Peter Levi, Virgil: A Life, 1997.

many of the heroes no longer had immortal blood in them. Certainly, Odysseus and Diomedes were more human, more like us, than the demi-gods, as it were, that preceded them.

And it is here that we see perhaps the full extent of Athene's power. It is Athene who, during the Trojan War, supports Diomedes in battle against Ares (in which Diomedes prevails), and who gives Diomedes special abilities enabling him to distinguish between gods and mortals on the battlefield. It is through Odysseus, who comes up with the ruse of the Trojan Horse, that she accomplishes the destruction of Troy, which all the fighting did not. Further, it is Athene who protects Odysseus on the journey home from Troy, including protection from the wrath of Poseidon who is the enemy of Odysseus. The protection extends to Odysseus's family – in particular his son, Telemachus, when she assumes the appearance of Mentor, who has died, to continue Telemachus' education. In other words, she is a 'mentor'.

Finally, in this brief account, there is something else that is astonishing about the goddess of wisdom, Athene: namely, that both Odysseus and Diomedes survive the Trojan War and according to most traditions (excepting that of Dante's, who was writing long after the events and in a different historical period) live into a ripe old age! Think about it: virtually all the Greek heroes (and certainly all the Trojan ones, except Aeneas) died violent and unpleasant deaths: Ajax the Great, Agamemnon, Achilles, and Patroclus. Menelaus did indeed survive to rule with Helen, but he is not generally considered one of their great warriors. Ajax the Lesser (there were two Ajaxes) did not survive and his end is instructive: he survived the war as a great warrior but like Odysseus had to return home; but unlike Odysseus who reverenced Athene, Ajax violated her sanctuary in the sacking of Troy, and thus earnt her implacable enmity and perished for his hubris.

What can we learn from these stories that help us today? First, that wisdom is a spirit that we need to embrace and seek out. This corresponds with the advice in the Bible: to seek out and find wisdom[100]. It is not passive; we need to be active about it. Put another way, we have no 'entitlement' to it, no rights to it, but we have to find it. It's a journey – an odyssey if you will.

This leads to the second point: by pursuing wisdom, we are all called to be heroes. Life requires heroism to confront the monsters, the apparitions, the fear, and all the other distortions that lead us to death. And being a hero, to be clear, from the perspective of the goddess, is not about brute strength and power: there is a strategy in it, a direction, it's goal-focused and has a higher purpose.

---

[100] Job 28 v12: "But where can wisdom be found? And where is the place of understanding?"

Third, we learn that we need to be persistent, and consistent and never give up on doing good (for she is the incorruptible virgin after all). Dr Johnson[101] said it this way: "Great works are not achieved by strength but by persistence." Or more recently, as the Hungarian-American physicist, Albert-Laszlo Barabas remarked[102], "Contrary to what many believe, your chances of success do not decline with age. With persistence, success can come at any age." These remarks are all indicators of a most powerful virtue: hope, for hope underpins wisdom, because by believing that wisdom will prevail – that order, justice, and sanity will prevail – we have hope and engender more of it. For more on hope, see Chapter 10.

In our current epoch where entitlements and rights supersede any sense of citizen's responsibilities and contributions, wisdom is ever more important. In a time when passiveness is all too apparent – time spent on mobile phones and virtual universes – committing to being a hero is ever more urgent, so we can carve out our own 'real' lives. And in a period when unjust laws, rules and regulations depress, demoralise and dehumanise us, we must practise the wisdom of Athene's persistence and stay true to our hopes of a better future that our own efforts will help inform. Studying wisdom, then, is not time idly spent.

Thus, having given an overview of Athene's wisdom – and from it, her power – let's move on to consider her cultivation of heroes in the next chapter.

---

[101] Commonly attributed to Dr Johnson.
[102] Albert-Laszlo Barabasi, cited in MoneyWeek, 11th January 2019.

Chapter 5:
Two Heroes Athene Helps: Perseus and Herakles

So far in this account of Greek myths, we have stuck to exploring the nature, and the adventures, of the great Olympians: the gods who created order and meaning wrenched from the chaos – or chaotic situation – that preceded them. So far as humans were concerned, the welfare of humanity depended on appeasing the gods and ensuring their help in combating the forces of chaos and disintegration, which were, of course, entirely synonymous with evil.

As a sidebar we should, perhaps, constantly keep this thought in mind when we review contemporary thinking in the light of Greek mythology: clearly, 'anarchy' (meaning 'without law') may sound 'good', hip or cool, but is self-evidently evil from the mythological perspective. For this battle against evil – aka: disorder – was never done, or fully completed; and so, from the heavens above and Tartarus below the Earth, more and more of the action happened on the Earth and directly involved human beings.

But what I mean by human beings and their involvement, is (in Greek mythology) semi-divine superheroes, if you will: mainly, sons of the gods[103]. And it is important at this point to note that the Greeks subscribed to a philosophy of degeneration or regression. Human beings became 'less' than they once were. One clear indicator of this across cultures, and including the Bible, is that longevity decreased. The Greeks thought of the Ages of Man in four stages: from the Golden Age of mankind to the Silver and Bronze and finally to Ages of Iron where evil is rampant. This concept or variants thereof is common to Greek, Roman, Hindu, Norse (the Ragnarok cycle), Zoroastrian, and Aztec mythologies.

It should be observed that the degeneration of humanity runs counter to modern ideology: indeed, perhaps the most obsessively held of modern mantras is the notion of 'progress' – that somehow human beings (through education and technology) are getting better. The philosopher, John Gray[104], made two trenchant comments on this situation: the rather dismissive, "Belief in progress is the Prozac of the thinking classes", and the profounder observation that "Postmodern thinkers may question scientific progress, but it is undoubtedly real. The illusion is in the belief that it can affect any fundamental alteration in the human condition". In other words, however much progress we may seem

---

[103] One very important exception to this generalisation is the case of Odysseus, who was fully human; and in a sense represents the last of the real Greek heroes and the weakest of them – but of course, because he is fully human with no divine parent, this makes his achievements all the more stunning and interesting.
[104] John Gray, *Heresies*, 2004.

to make scientifically and technologically, human nature and the human condition remain resolutely what it always was: in Greek terms, this means mortal, vulnerable, and under the jurisdiction of the natural order and of the gods more specifically.

A further implication of all this is this: the gods themselves are in a hierarchy, and we are in a hierarchy beneath them, and animals are in a hierarchy beneath us, and so on. Hierarchy, therefore, is endemic, inevitable and 'right' – right operationally (as in life is made possible by it), but also in a moral sense, since the hierarchy enables and sustains order. This view is widespread and very ancient. We have already cited Jordan B Peterson's view on the 'dominance' hierarchy, but to take a culture a breath-taking distance away from the Greeks, the Chinese believed it, for as Adrian Furnham[105] remarked: "The Chinese believe hierarchies and inequalities are natural, necessary and inevitable. It is better and more efficient to accept inequality than to attempt to impose equality, which leads to chaos" – imposing 'equality' leads to chaos! Philosophies and their concomitant political organisations that attempt to impose 'equality', therefore, are evil because they engender chaos.

With these thoughts in mind, then, let's return to our Greek heroes who defeat disorder and evil, and so who promote life and liberty within the cosmic framework that is in its nature hierarchical. First up is Perseus.

Perseus is one of the greatest Greek heroes; and he was the great-grandfather of the most famous of them all, Herakles. But unlike Herakles and most of the others, Perseus is an intriguingly bland sort of hero. We learn little about his inner psyche, and – remarkably - unlike most of the other heroes, once he falls in love with the beautiful Andromeda, marries her, then he stays in love. Compare that with, say, Odysseus, who loved Penelope, but ... along the way...Circe, et. al.! Perseus is a real, regular guy then; except ... his destiny is to be a hero.

As an awkward young man, trying to advance in the world, Perseus tries to get an invitation to the king's social event of the year. A horse is the admission fee, but rashly Perseus offers to provide Medusa's head. Actually, as with many young men, he has no idea how he would go about getting that head, even where it is located, and how he would overcome the formidable obstacle of Medusa herself resisting his efforts to decapitate her! But the king accepts the offer because he has designs on Perseus' mother - and who wants a protective, big teenager lolling around?

At this point we need to keep in mind a few extra facts about this narrative. First, that Perseus is the son of Zeus, begotten in a

---

[105] Adrian Furnham, *The Psychology of Behaviour at Work: The Individual in the Organization*, 2005.

shower of gold upon Danae. Thus, he has pedigree and a destiny to continue Zeus's work. This work is no less than maintaining the fragile stability of the cosmos – its order, structure, purpose. Who then is Medusa whom he has promised to decapitate?

Medusa ('Queen') is one of three Gorgons. Her sisters, Stheno ('Strength') and Euryale ('Wide-Jump') are immortal, but Medusa is not. However, the terrifying aspect of Medusa is not just her dire appearance, including snakes for hair, but the fact that one glance from her petrifies organic matter into stone. The etymology of petrify here is, of course, directly relevant: when we are petrified, we mean we are terrified – or fearful – to such an extent that we are immobilised; but the word 'petrify' comes from the Greek word meaning stone or rock.

Thus, one of the evils that lead to breakdown and disorder and death is fear – or more precisely the terror that turns us to stone. If we think about it, the ability to turn all living matter into mineral form, as Medusa does, undermines the cosmos and would ultimately lead to its extinction; for all living creatures would be stone. Thus, it is necessary to the divine order that Medusa be destroyed. In our modern conception of fear, we say that it is responsible for one of the 3 Fs in response – Fight, Flight or Freeze. Clearly, the freeze is the worst state of all since it paralyses all action, literally petrifying us. As JG Ballard observed in his novel, The Drowned World, 'Nothing endures for so long as fear', and being a rock perfectly captures that desperate, duration-less state. Perseus is a hero because he is a master over terror.

So it is that Perseus is befriended by two of the most powerful Olympians - favourite children of Zeus - the goddess of wisdom, Athene, and the messenger god, the god of liminal spaces, Hermes. Both of whom we have already met; and who would want to help Perseus for one obvious reason: they are half-siblings, since Zeus has fathered them all. Through them Perseus is shown the 'way' and ultimately equipped with five necessary weapons: Hades' Cap of invisibility, the winged sandals of Hermes, a special bag (kibisis) that can contain the severed head (without turning to stone itself), an adamantine blade that can cut anything, and a shield that can be polished into a mirror.

But being a 'master of terror' is not some automatic switch one turns on; a lot of preparation is necessary. Consider: first, that the cause is right and that the gods are behind you, for then doubt cannot assail you, doubt being the bridgehead to fear. Second, that you move with lightning speed (winged sandals), that you become invisible (Cap of Hades) as opposed to proclaiming your movements, that you know the nature of your enemy and avoid collateral damage (the kibisis), and that you have a weapon (adamantine blade) effective enough to cut through the enemy. And this is why, of course, the goddess Athene is so important: she, who advises Perseus, is wisdom and part of that wisdom is foresight. It is worth mentioning that despite the support of the great gods, Ares, Apollo and Aphrodite, Troy fell because, for one thing, Athene is against them; she gives Odysseus the strategic idea of the 'Trojan Horse', which proves fateful.

The above list for mastering terror is also a menu for warfare against evil: is our cause just? What about our timing? Speed stuns. Cloak yourself, your intentions, your movements in secrecy. Know your enemy and their whereabouts. Avoid collateral damage in order to pre-empt pyrrhic victories. Have weapons that are really effective and lethal. Perhaps this doesn't include all 12 or so principles of war[106], but it certainly vividly demonstrates some of their most important aspects.

Medusa represents a kind of terror that not only clouds the mind, but also the vision: one cannot look at her without being overcome. In one sense the myth of Perseus is a myth of maturation. To become adults, we have to face the darkest aspects of our existence and not fall under the spell of its petrifying negativity. And to do this we need the final weapon, the reflecting shield. We have to look, we have to see, which means to understand – but to do so in a way in which we do not partake of its reality. If we remember the Garden of Eden problem: the eating of the fruit of good and evil meant not just that they 'knew' good and evil academically, but that they became evil as a direct experiential result of the eating. So here: to directly look at the physical 'thing' itself is to incorporate it into one's own being, and is to become terror or fear itself. At that point, the heart stops and we become stone. However, the shield reflects, and through it we can see an inversion of what 'is' – like studying a photograph of an atrocity; but knowing it's not real means we are not caught up in its horror. It creates a distance between us and the 'thing' – the petrifying 'thing'. In this way Perseus can move towards fear and destroy her with one, decisive blow.

Thus, dealing with fear requires foresight, preparation and decisive action. Another way of expressing the final action, of course, is what we now might call 're-framing'[107] fear. The shield reframes what we are seeing, and in this way enables us to deal with it because it protects us – as shields should do.

Two small but significant extra points emerge from this

---

[106] There are various accounts and lists of the principles of war, but they invariably include the following principles: Objective, Offensive, Mass, Economy of Force, Manoeuvre, Unity of Command, Security, Surprise, Simplicity, Flexibility and Adaptability, Morale and Psychological Operations.

[107] Reframing is a powerful Neuro-Linguistic Programming (NLP) technique used to alter the way individuals perceive a situation, thought, or behaviour by changing its meaning or context. The idea is to shift one's perspective in a way that opens up new, more empowering ways of thinking or behaving.

story. The first is that the death of Medusa immediately unleashes two living horses from her blood, Chrysaor and Pegasus. The latter is the most famous – and winged – horse in history. And that might give us pause for thought: the king wanted a horse as the price of admission to his party; it was a horse that led to Troy's destruction; and now a winged horse appears. Poseidon, god of the sea and earthquakes, and of all turbulent and disturbing emotions (for water represents emotion), was also god of horses. He is the father of Medusa! What we are witnessing is the symbolism by which horses have always represented transcendence for human beings: through horses we can go beyond our own limits of speed and strength. Poseidon gifted horses to humans, but Athene gifted the bridle to enable us to contain them effectively. Here with the release of Pegasus we have the ultimate in going 'beyond'. Once we have defeated our fear, our terror, we too can fly – be heroes and heroines.

Second, in the aftermath of this, Athene attaches Medusa's head to her own battle shield going into war. It was, naturally enough, to terrify her enemies. Here we have god-like intelligence unaffected by fear and terror and using it strategically against those who oppose her. To be like this in the midst of war and chaos is perhaps truly to have god-like powers. At this point we are not fearing fear; we are turning fear into an ally. One is reminded at this point of fairly recent history and President FD Roosevelt who presciently in his first Inaugural Address in 1933 said, "So, first of all, let me assert my firm belief that the only thing we have to fear is…fear itself — nameless, unreasoning, unjustified terror which paralyzes needed efforts to convert retreat into advance." This is what Perseus is countering.

There is, however, a certain irony in all this if we return to the pre-story of the three Gorgons: they claimed to be more beautiful than Athene, which hubris could not be forgiven; so, Athene disfigured them into the ugly beings that they became. But Wisdom – Athene - uses Medusa's head as part of her shield – projecting the 'terror of mind' going into battle against her enemies: in short, the hubris has been punished by Athene using Perseus, and then converted into a weapon the goddess uses against others exhibiting hubris. Hubris, in other words, can become a weapon to defeat itself if – like Athene – we think strategically.

Athene, then, was central to the success of Perseus in his mission to destroy Medusa and her evil 'property/power' of turning organic matter to stone: a property, which if left unchecked, might well destroy all of human life. Actually, we shall consider exactly this property again – and its menace to life – in chapter 7 when we look at the story of Midas and his famous touch, which turned everything to gold. Initially, of course, Midas was very happy about this, but as he learnt: this 'property' is anti-life and promotes disorder.

To return to the mortal heroes, the greatest of them all was Herakles[108], the great grandson of Perseus, and also – if you will! – a half-brother because Zeus too was his father. Attempting to tell the full story of Herakles would be a book in itself and so I would like to focus on just one of his mythical exploits which seems very relevant to the world today.

Famously, Herakles undertook his 12 Labours, each of them is highly significant, and given that there are 12 we may safely assume they are and were associated with the heavenly bodies, or the Zodiac. For example, his first exploit was to destroy the Nemean Lion, which clearly references the constellation of Leo. His second exploit, which is what I wish to review, is to take-out the Hydra (which like the precession of the equinox goes in reverse order every 2000 years, and so links to the constellation of Cancer: a crab is involved in the tale!). I say 'take-out', not destroy because in an important sense the Hydra cannot be destroyed as we shall see.

So, the story of the Lernaean Hydra, or just the Hydra, is that of a snake-like monster who in the most authoritative sources had nine heads, one of which was immortal. On top of which the creature's breath was a lethal poison and it spat a venom so deadly that there was no cure for it. Hydra was the offspring of the loathsome monster, Echidna, who mated with the even more ferocious Typhon. It was Typhon who almost defeated the king of the gods himself, Zeus, and in doing so would have destroyed the whole created order if it had been successful. The Hydra lived beside Lake Lerna, guarding an ominous gate leading to the underworld.

Thus, it should not surprise us that just as the king of heaven had fought and defeated the Typhon monster in the upper world, so here below on Earth, it fell to his son, the human hero, Herakles, to defeat Typhon's offspring, the Hydra; and this came about as a result of the second Labour that he was ordered to do by the treacherous and weak king Eurystheus. Eurytheus didn't really care about the Hydra one way or the other: his real objective in setting all twelve of the famous Labours was for Herakles himself to be destroyed; for each of the Labours became increasingly difficult and impossible to achieve. But, of course, Herakles was half-human, half-divine; his father was Zeus; this was no ordinary man!

But even being half-divine proved not quite enough in this instance for Herakles to be able to overcome the Hydra, at least on his own; for as he cut off or clubbed each head to death, another two would sprout in its place. The Hydra thus became more powerful, and Herakles had to retire. And the Hydra herself was not alone:

---

[108] A point of dispute when we come to consider Odysseus in chapters 11 and 12!

the Queen of Heaven (Hera) who hated Herakles, ordered a giant crab to attack him from the rear. Fortunately, however, Herakles was accompanied by Iolaos, his nephew, and together – resuming the fight - as Herakles destroyed one head, and before it could regenerate into two, Iolaos would sear the neck stump with a red-hot brand and thus prevent it growing again. Eventually, as one head after another died, the creature too did, leaving only the immortal head. These Herakles chopped off and buried by the roadside. The Hydra, then, was defeated and dead. (Herakles also had peremptorily crushed the crab and Hera set it in the sky to commemorate its contribution).

So, what is the relevance of this story for us? The Hydra, I think, is symbolic of mankind's efforts (often monstrous!) to solve its problems; we might call this revisiting our philosophy of 'progress'; and in particular its 'problem-solving' capacities, especially via science and technology. Take, for example, in the mid-20th century, the pesticide DDT was widely used to combat mosquito populations and reduce the spread of malaria. While it initially proved effective, the long-term environmental consequences were devastating. DDT entered ecosystems and accumulated in the tissues of animals, especially birds. It caused eggshell thinning, leading to massive declines in bird populations, including the American bald eagle, which nearly went extinct. The attempt to save human lives from malaria inadvertently led to severe environmental damage and the near-extinction of species.

Or take how in the 2000s, many countries, including the United States, introduced biofuel mandates to reduce greenhouse gas emissions and combat climate change. These mandates encouraged the use of corn and other crops to produce ethanol and biodiesel, providing more eco-friendly energy alternatives to fossil fuels. However, the unintended consequence was that diverting large amounts of crops to fuel production reduced the global supply of food, driving up food prices. This disproportionately affected poorer populations, leading to food shortages and unrest in various parts of the world, such as the 2007–2008 global food crisis.

Even more recently[109] we read of vaccines to save lives, but immediately the opposite occurs – another head of the Hydra pops up, just when we thought we'd nailed the problem. A law of unintended consequences occurs. But not only unintended, but unforeseen too. As G.K. Chesterton observed[110], "Science invents conveniences by design and inconveniences by accident."

---

[109] The Epoch Times, 1/18/2021: "Officials in Norway said they are investigating the deaths of about two dozen elderly patients who received the Pfizer/BioNTech vaccine and are looking into the prospect that adverse reactions to the vaccine 'may have contributed to a fatal outcome in some frail patients'." In attempting to save people's lives, they kill them!
[110] Cited by Bob Seidensticker, Future Hype, 2006.

Even, apparently, the creation of self-evidently brilliant new technologies, on reflection, seem to carry a sting in their tail, or – to continue our metaphor – generate a new Hydra's head that attacks us somehow. For example, who could argue that the invention of the alphabet and writing was a great new technology? Have we not been the beneficiaries of its power ever since? Indeed, without it, it is difficult to conceive of how any learning, much less science, could ever have evolved. Yet, it was Socrates[111] who said, "The discovery of the alphabet will create forgetfulness in the learner's soul, because they will not use their memories; they will trust the external written characters and not remember of themselves."

Of course, it may be thought now that the weakening of the memory is a small price to pay for the ability to be able to write, record and transmit information to posterity in the way that writing has enabled. But the trouble is, whereas there are very small Hydras, there are also very large ones, especially since the start of the Industrial Revolution in the Nineteenth century. We have become so dependent on technologies that we are scarcely aware of our dependencies ... until something goes wrong; like, for example, Covid-19. Then suddenly we become all too aware that globalisation – which in the 1990s we were told was unstoppable, inevitable and more or less wholly beneficial – has some serious downsides: mass traveling, spreading the virus, supply-chains which are vulnerable, and a particularly negative effect on the poorest in society. And more beside: if we consider the officials in Norway's investigation[112], we may be on the brink of discovering that the so-called safe vaccines have not really been tested sufficiently. As Carl Sagan said, "We live in a society exquisitely dependent on science and technology, in which hardly anyone knows anything about science and technology". Unlike Herakles, we are all disempowered consumers who have to take what we are given.

Given all this – and the Hydras of nuclear power, biological experimentation (of which Covid itself may well be a consequence), pollution, global-warming and so on – we have to ask: what can be done about it? Does the myth give us a clue? The answer is yes; it does.

We have to set a hero (or heroine) up to fight against these Hydras. But the essence of the hero is that he is semi-divine; and the point of this is that solving human problems is at least half a spiritual matter, for that is what 'divine' means. Science and technology on their own are not going to solve our problems; they cannot solve our problems! As Robert Pirsig[113] commented, "What's

---

[111] Plato's Phaedra c. 370 BC.
[112] Ibid note v
[113] Robert Pirsig, Zen and the Art of Motorcycle Maintenance, 1974.

wrong with technology is that it's not connected in any real way with matters of the spirit and the heart. And so it does blind, ugly things quite by accident and gets hated for that." By its very nature, technology is spiritless; but Herakles is not, he is semi-divine and semi-human. And notice, too, Herakles works with another human being, and they work as a team to overcome The Hydra.

In his fascinating book, Future Hype, Bob Seidensticker talks about 'wicked problems', and these are what I call The Hydra: "Wicked problems have complex cause-and-effect relationships, include human interaction, and simply inherently incomplete information. They require compromises. ... When there is a big difference between how something works in the lab, in academia, on paper, or in one's head and how it works in the real world and affects real people, you know you are dealing with a wicked problem."

It is, therefore, the re-introduction of what is human and spiritual into combatting the problems of our time which is of the essence; only in this way can further Hydras be prevented. But sadly, there is yet another Hydra to confront in the myth; because, even for Herakles, there was a 'Hydra' that he did not foresee.

You will remember that he lopped off the immortal Hydra's head as well, and buried it. The burial is significant in that the immortal part of this evil cannot be killed – evil, in other words, continues to persist whatever we – as heroes – do to excise it. Vigilance, then, is absolutely necessary, for just when we think we have eliminated evil, we have not: it is buried somewhere and will re-emerge in another form. All utopian thinking, then, is revealed by this myth to be false – and a lot of 'academic' thinking too. A splendid example is Francis Fukuyama[114] and his now absurd-looking argument in the 1990s that we had reached the 'end of history', and the triumph and eventual universalization of Western liberal democracy meant all was well in the world forever! But there is more.

Herakles, before burying the immortal head, took an ample supply of its poisoned venom with which to tip his arrows – making them fatal, the merest graze would kill any living being. He killed many enemies this way. But finally, he was caught by the technology himself: the poison was infused into a shirt that his wife inadvertently supplied him with, and he died in agony. Even the great Herakles could not escape the Hydra – far better for him, perhaps, to really have buried the technology than to think he could actually use it for his own ends. It rather reminds one of The Lord of the Rings[115], and the ring of power which always betrayed those

---

[114] The End of History and the Last Man, 1992.
[115] JRR Tolkien, The Lord of the Rings, 1954.

who sought to wield it (excepting its maker, the Dark Lord). To use the weapons of the enemy can be seriously problematic!

We need more heroes in the world today to fight the Hydras that are continually multiplying; and we need alongside it a spiritual awareness that transcends mere materialism.

Chapter 6:
Orpheus and Eurydice and the Descent into Hell

As we reach the midpoint of this book it seems appropriate – as we have already covered some aspects of the gods in heaven and the heroes on Earth - to dwell on what the Greeks called katabasis: the descent into hell. This 'other' place, which is part of the structure of the Cosmos, and which is necessary for the divine order to be sustainable, appears – unlike Heaven and Earth – highly undesirable. But before looking at what the Greeks meant by hell, it's a good idea to think about how we view it nowadays, since this has important implications for how we interpret the myths.

Essentially, the modern Western world does not believe in the existence of hell, if by hell we mean the reality of some metaphysical zone or place that succeeds mortal life and to which humans are destined to go after their deaths. Aside from the persistent craze for video games and films which do depict 'hell' as a place of after-life, we tend to mean nowadays hell is … hell-on-earth. War breaks out in Ukraine or Somalia or Gaza and we say it is 'hell' there, meaning hell-on-earth. Perhaps the greatest poem written during World War I was Wilfred Owen's 'Strange Meeting' in which combatants on the Western Front – a place universally described and depicted as hell – meet in an eerie, hell-like liminal space after their deaths.

But it is not just being at war that creates hell. Thomas Merton[116] made the general observation that "If we follow nothing but our natures, our own philosophies, our own level of ethics, we will end up in hell." There is, if you like, a sort of necessity about hell; it's as if it were, or is, a place where all the loose ends of creation are tied up. In other words, all the disorder, all the evil that is not reconciled to and in the processes of living, becomes permanently knotted and displaced elsewhere where that disorder, that evil, can no longer threaten life and the living. The sense of 'knottedness' and 'permanence' mean that "…nothing is harder than to come back from hell.[117]" Why? Because to come back from hell – which in the case of humans means to come back from the dead – means to undo the cosmos, it means to displace order with disorder, it means to give evil full license to propagate itself. This is why, when the great medic of antiquity, Aesculapius (see chapter 2), actually starting raising the dead (even though on behalf of the great goddess, Artemis, daughter of Zeus), Zeus struck him dead to prevent this further incursion into the structure of the cosmos.

We might think that having the healing powers to bring

---

[116] Thomas Merton, The Seven Storey Mountain, 1948.
[117] Neel Burton, *The Meaning of Myth*, 2021. Also, "The exit from Hell is always difficult" from Percy Harrison Faucett, cited in *The Lost City of Z*, David Grann, 2009.

back the dead is a good thing; but the Greek myths tell us otherwise, and so would definitely consider modern attempts to do this utterly hubristic. Currently we learn that the Californian-based Bryan Johnson[118] spends some $2M a year on his 'Project Blueprint' to stay young and prevent death!

We, of course, in the West, though official Christianity is in decline, inherit our historic view of hell from its traditions. And, amusingly, as the American astronaut Frank Borman[119], expressed it, "Capitalism without bankruptcy is like Christianity without Hell." But here's the rub: the concept of hell is unpopular to the exact degree that freedom of the will is unpopular - today we all want to be victims. Or as Prue Shaw[120] explains it: "… if you believe in freedom of the human will, and in God, you must believe in the possibility of the human being turning away from God eternally. Hence the logic of Hell." And hence the logic of socialism in which there are no bankruptcies; and the logic of some of the personal development movements in which there are no failures; and the increasing 'logic' of believing anybody can be anything they want, no matter what 'reality' says to the contrary. But as Thomas Sowell[121] observed: "Reality is not optional."

However, despite the wisdom of Sowell, there has been for over a century, a drift towards preferring nice, easy options, and nice easy beliefs, rather taking on board personal responsibility and the hard idea that we are accountable in some deep metaphysical way to some transcendental reality that the Greek myths and the Christian tradition – in their different ways – all point to. But it's not just the Greeks and Christians who have this belief in hell: virtually all civilisations have had it from the beginning. The Egyptians, the Assyrians, the Babylonians and every culture that is a culture seems to believe in the afterlife, contacting the dead, ancestor-worship and the reality of hell. Indeed, even a religion such as Buddhism, which many claim to have no transcendental god/God, seems to believe in hell: only they call it reincarnation! For what is reincarnation but – if you are evil, if you do not escape what they call samsara[122] –a perpetual form of hell as you return again and again in lower life forms? Peter Levi in his book on Virgil[123] put it quite magnificently this way: "… belief in punishment in hell was already old and deeply rooted – … Hell is twice as deep as the sky is high above Mount Olympus." Twice as deep as heaven

---

[118] Bryan Johnson, https://en.wikipedia.org/wiki/Bryan_Johnson
[119] Frank Borman, cited from Forbes, Money Week 19th of January 2024.
[120] Prue Shaw, Reading Dante, 2014.
[121] Thomas Sowell, Is Reality Optional? And Other Essays, 1993.
[122] Samsara refers to the cycle of birth, death, and rebirth that all beings are trapped in, driven by ignorance, desire, and karma. It is often depicted as a cycle of suffering (dukkha), where individuals move through different states of existence, experiencing various forms of life, such as humans, animals, gods, or spirits, based on their past actions (karma).
[123] Peter Levi, Virgil, A Life, 1997.

is high! Wow! What this suggests is that the foundations of the cosmos are built on much more 'material' – dense materials - than we can ever visibly see. Put another way: hell is the reality that sustains life!

So, what was the Greek conception of hell via its myths? Interestingly, the Greek myths depict two levels of hell. In Greek mythology, Hades and Tartarus refer to two distinct places and deities, although both are associated with the underworld. Hades as a place is sometimes used interchangeably with the name of the god, Hades (Pluto in Latin), who rules there. This underworld is where the souls of the dead go after death. It is divided into different sections, including the Elysian Fields (for the virtuous) and Asphodel Meadows (for ordinary souls).

The realm of Hades is not necessarily a place of punishment for all, although some are punished there, but it is seen rather as where souls exist after death. However, that said, it is not a pleasant place to be; as Odysseus[124] discovers, when he meets Achilles in the underworld: "Nay, glorious Odysseus," answered Achilles, "speak not soothingly to me of death. I would rather be a paid servant in a poor man's house and be above ground than king of kings among the dead."

Tartarus is a specific, deeper region within the underworld, and for good reason is considered the darkest, most hellish part of Hades. It serves as a dungeon of torment for the wicked and a prison for the Titans (those gods who were overthrown by Zeus and the Olympians). It is essentially a place of punishment. Some myths describe Tartarus as a primordial force or entity, but it is primarily known as the prison for those who defy the gods. It is hell at its most extreme. Virgil vividly describes it in Book 6 of his Aeneid: Tartarus is described as a vast, terrifying place, enclosed by a high wall and surrounded by the river Phlegethon, which flows with fire. The entrance is guarded by a Hydra (an evil entity we met in Chapter 5!) with fifty black mouths. Inside, souls are punished for their crimes, such as betrayal, greed, and impiety. In other words, the wicked are punished, and there is a moral law running through the cosmos, which one disobeys at one's peril.

For our purposes now, I think we can consider hell as one entity: subdivisions within it, certainly, but a place where one does not really want to go! As we said before, and as long ago Jung warned us: what we have ignored or denied inwardly will then manifest itself outwardly, that is, in the 'real' world; it will come upon us, as it were, like our fate. The Greeks were very familiar with this idea and had a number of words for it: 'moirai' or fate, 'dike' or justice, and 'nemesis' or 'consequential retribution'. The American

---

[124] The Odyssey, book 11, translated by Samuel Butler, 1900.

psychotherapist James Hollis[125] perceptively observed that "our hubristic belief that we are in control of ourselves and nature only makes us more unconscious of what is at work within us". And what is that? Our souls - or if we don't like that old-fashioned word - our true Self[126].

But soul is good enough, for when we use that word, we recall all its cultural associations; and we remember too that in all cultures throughout history there has always been an awareness that the soul of a human being is the most precious thing we have, that nothing can be given in exchange[127] for it, and that to lose one's soul is to enter into a shadowy domain generally known as hell; and this condition, which is permanent, involves total and absolute loss of true identity. To lose one's soul - ah! There's the rub. Atheists, materialists, secularists, humanists all really can't see the point of what they see as over-dramatic talk, for how can one lose that which doesn't exist? Furthermore, hell is just a chimera to frighten children, isn't it?

It would be comforting to think so, but really the facts suggest otherwise. One fact we have already alluded to: that virtually all cultures everywhere have stories and myths about the soul and, indeed, about hell. I take the view that people are not stupid, not sheep who are easily led, but that much if not most of their beliefs and practices stem from their real-world experiences. Thus, if the myths have consistently emerged surrounding these topics, then it is because they are sourced from some underlying reality that collectively humanity has understood as real.

Second, by way of 'facts', we do see so many people alive now who, though not dead, are in 'hell': gripped by addictions, compulsions and sufferings that represent nothing so much as the depictions of 'life' in hell that the Greeks have left us. Who has not, for example, witnessed some 'living' Sisyphus[128], rolling their boulder up a hill, only for it to roll down, and then doing it again ad infinitum - and all to no end? We know these people, don't we? This happens long before many become old and get stuck in care homes. Why do they do it? What caused this catastrophe in their lives? Why, we ask; and, of course, like evil itself, there is no why – indeed,

---

[125] James Hollis, Finding Meaning in the Second Half of Life, 2006.
[126] Allan Bloom put it thus: "To sum up, the self is the modern substitute for the soul" - The Closing of the American Mind, 1987.
[127] The key text here is from Christ: "For what good will it do a person if he gains the whole world, but forfeits his soul? Or what will a person give in exchange for his soul?" Matthew 16:26, NASB. This is echoed recently by Patrick Harpur, A Complete Guide to the Soul, 2010: "Even if we are not specifically religious, we can all still resonate with the notion that there is some part of us which should not be sold, betrayed or lost at any cost."
[128] Sisyphus was condemned to Tartarus for various crimes, including cheating death! His punishment was to eternally push a large boulder up a hill, only for it to roll back down every time he neared the top, forcing him to start over endlessly.

all rationality is gone. The creative Word – the divine Logos[129] – has truly crashed for some, and the void (old Chaos, as Milton[130] called it) has returned.

Our Western society has coined its own special word to describe this state of its citizens; and at the same time as coining the term has managed to avoid any theological taint that might suggest we are under some supernatural curse: 'alienation'. That has become our modern myth (note, incidentally, the root of the word: we prefer to believe in aliens that we virtually have no evidence of, rather than supernatural realities, for which we do): some sort of sociological explanation as to why people are alienated from their environments, from society and even from each other. Note, also, two other supplementary modern myths: that sociology is some sort of science, and that science can and will explain this condition and – with enough further research – resolve it. In the myth as it currently runs, we can expect the word 'education' (along with its cousin 'progress') to pop up soon, and all will be well.

For now, let us consider one of the ancient myths that, indirectly, explains myth itself! This most compelling myth is that of Orpheus; it has much to teach us about the nature of the things, especially the nature of the cosmos or what I might now call the universe: the uni (one) - verse (song or poem). What does this mean or point to? That the whole of creation is a work of art! Imagine that – everything, from the beginning (according to science, on its current estimate, 13.7 billion years ago) till now, is dynamic art, or is art in motion. And if that is true, as our own naming indicates, how much more must each individual life be part of that work of art? Indeed, there is a requirement (the moral imperative, or the law within) for every one of us to make our life a work of art. The word 'make' here is also highly significant, for that is what the word 'poet' etymologically means: poets are makers. So, we are back to 'verse' again, the one verse. Hell, then, is that condition where we refuse to collaborate on creating that poem, that song, that is the meaning of the universe. In Cocteau's Orpheus, seeing those in hell, Orpheus asks, 'Are these people alive?' And Heurtebise[131] answers, 'They think they are.' Myths speak sometimes of the delusions of the human mind, and in the case of hell of being trapped within the delusion.

Orpheus (meaning 'darkness or fatherless/so orphan') is the poet and singer, and son of the god Apollo, who is the god of light, poetry and healing. Orpheus's wife, Eurydice (meaning 'deep justice' – we met the word 'dike' earlier), whom he dearly loves, is

---

[129] The divine Logos here refers to the opening chapter of John's gospel where the Word (Logos) is said to be in the beginning with God and is God. The word Logos means Word and also Meaning.
[130] John Milton, *Paradise Lost*, 1674 edition, book 2.
[131] Cited in Ann Wroe, Orpheus, 2011

bitten by a snake and dies. Grief-stricken, Orpheus, whose words and music can move even rocks and stones, decides to venture into hell, where the dead are, and entreat Hades, the god of the dead, to release her back into the realm of the living.

Interestingly, as a sidebar, Hades is hell's Greek name, but it is Pluto in Roman; from which we get the word 'plutocrat' - for because Pluto receives all the dead, and all die, he is said to be the richest of the gods. So, we have here a faint echo of the connection between money and death, as with the Biblical injunction[132] that the love of money is the root of much evil.

But two things need observing at this point: first, that Eurydice dies via a snake bite. Why a snake? What does a snake - or serpent - remind us of? Yes, the Garden of Eden, another 'myth'. Snakes are symbols of knowledge or wisdom. We murder to dissect, as Wordsworth[133] said, and the Tree of Knowledge destroys us; it deceives us into thinking we are gods when we are not.

Second, who is Eurydice anyway? His wife? Yes, in one sense, because she is the most beautiful and lovely person in the world, but no: at a deeper level Eurydice is Orpheus's own soul - the true beloved, the thing most precious in Eastern and Western spiritual traditions - the pearl of great price. She is the anima to his masculine identity.

Orpheus, then, finds the entrance and begins the long descent. All the difficulties and terrors he encounters he defeats and charms with his poetry and song. Two remarkable things occur on the way down: first, he descends further and deeper into hell than any other Greek hero, including Herakles - the power of his music and poetry is more potent than all the physical weapons and overwhelming strength of the traditional heroes. As Ann Wroe[134] once commented: "For as the works of wisdom surpass in dignity and power the works of strength, so the labour of Orpheus surpasses the labours of Hercules." And, as he plays, the torments of hell are suspended - even the damned stopped what they were senselessly doing and their rationality begins to return, and this includes those in Tartarus. Such is the power of beauty; everything – 'things' – come alive again as the heavenly music of his lyre reconnects them to their divine, and so living, origin. Here, hell ends, except ...

At last, he arrives in the very throne room of hell itself and stands before Hades, the King, and Persephone, the queen. And so,

---

[132] "For the love of money is a root of all sorts of evil, and some by longing for it have wandered away from the faith and pierced themselves with many griefs."1 Timothy 6:10 (NASB).
[133] William Wordsworth, The Lyrical Ballads, 1798, and his poem, The Tables Turned:
"Sweet is the lore which Nature brings;
Our meddling intellect
Misshapes the beauteous forms of things—
We murder to dissect."
[134] Ann Wroe, ibid.

a third, remarkable phenomenon occurs: listening to Orpheus' music, Hades sheds a tear (a tear pitch-black as tar) for the first and only time in Greek mythology. The music moves even death, and Hades agrees as a reward to allow Eurydice to return on one condition: that Eurydice follow behind Orpheus and that he does not look back to see her until he reaches the light.

Orpheus agrees and sets off to return. Facts – things – knowledge have killed his soul, but now his imagination expressed through his singing has soared and enabled him to make a pact with Death's self, and he can return, soul restored. We see here the very limit of human power – a deal with the god.

Now he has the promise of Eurydice; but to convert that into a living reality requires that Orpheus believes the word of the god: is she really following behind or will he find he has been tricked when he reaches the surface world again? And also, that he does not look back on the soul directly in the unreal world of hell. I say 'unreal' because that is how death seems to us, and hell too; but in another way, hell is more real than the world we live in now. The world we live in now changes and passes away – we are but grass[135] that flourishes and then is gone. But the point of the underworld is its eternal nature: there we are what we have become, forever. What could be more real than that? Indeed, as Dante's character, Capocchio, the counterfeiter, says, in Clive James recent translation[136]: "I did well/ In life. But everything is real in Hell".

And this is why this myth is the myth of myths themselves; for the condition for the return of the soul is that we do not look back. The 'not looking back' easily reminds us of the story of Lot's wife[137]: who in looking back was turned into a pillar of salt. But in that story the 'sin' of the looking back seems primarily to do with the ingratitude of the wife towards the deliverance that God had provided; in some real way we sense that the looking back for her was with a passion for the old life and without gratitude either for their escape or for the new life to come. Here, I think, with Orpheus, it is not so much the 'looking back' as what looking back involves: namely: directly viewing the object – indeed, the act of viewing, and seeking out, the person as an object to view (so objectifying) is to convert it/her to an object, to a fact, to a piece of knowledge. The very thing that killed Eurydice, via the snake, in the first place! And will remember from chapter 5, that Perseus was only able to kill Medusa by not looking directly at her.

---

[135] "As for man, his days are like grass;
As a flower of the field, so he flourishes.
When the wind has passed over it, it is no more,
And its place acknowledges it no longer." Psalm 103:15-16. (NASB)
[136] Clive James, Dante: *The Divine Comedy*, Inferno, Canto 29, 2013.
[137] "But Lot's wife, from behind him, looked back, and she became a pillar of salt." Genesis, 19.26.

When the imagination (the poet/singer in us all) views anything, it does not do it directly, for that would be simply to itemise it. No, the imagination sees – comprehends as in a vision - the invisible world where everything comes alive. If this seems strange, then consider how we experience it all the time: most obviously in our dreams where anything and everything comes alive, sometimes delightfully, but oftentimes frighteningly too. Thus, we cannot look directly at our own souls, at least whilst in the land of living. To look at our own souls would be like asking our eyes to look at our eyes: that is impossible, except by using a mirror or shield so that we receive reflections of what reality is. We can only look at our souls indirectly. And this is exactly what myths do: they tell us indirectly the most important truths in the universe, but because they do so indirectly, we mostly miss the meaning, and fail to grasp the import. So, it just becomes a story, of greater or lesser interest.

This myth, then, reveals a profound truth: mankind is in search of his/her soul that was lost long ago in some aboriginal catastrophe. Interestingly, in returning without Eurydice to the surface – to the superficial – without his soul, it is only a matter of time before Orpheus is slain, torn apart, dismembered by the Thracian women. Why? Because they cannot accept in their wine-drenched revelry that a human being can grieve for the love of their life – their soul – and prefer it perpetually before the Thracian's superficial hedonism; and this too is indicative of the ongoing relationship between materialists and those spiritually oriented. (Materialists hate religion and spirituality not because, as they like to claim, of historical abuses in the name of religion, but because all spiritual understandings displace mankind's ego from the centre of the universe, and this – in the cant of our times, replacing right and wrong - is 'unacceptable'). But in any case, without the soul the body dies, for the soul is the immortal part. Each one of us, therefore, has to accept the challenge – to find our soul and to live not by being born (that is simply naturalistic), but by first having come back from the dead (which is to say, being born again).

The myth of Orpheus seems not to end well, but actually we sense in it a destiny, a nobility, a grandeur, and a truth – for what is our/my song that we must sing in order to facilitate the descent? That is what we are searching for; till we find it, the myth of Orpheus suggests we may barely be alive.

We shall return to the myth of searching for, returning to our own soul when we consider the story of Odysseus in chapters 11 and 12.

Chapter 7:
Two Cautionary Tales – Midas and Narcissus

We have so far looked at four of the great gods of Greek mythology, and their achievements in ordering the cosmos; also, we have considered the works of three semi-divine heroes, Perseus, Herakles and Orpheus, who have continued the activities of their divine fathers in propagating good and defeating evil in the world, according to the supernal rules that Zeus established. Our theme remains the same, but now we consider it from the point of view, not of heroes, but of weak humans – perhaps some more like 'Us' - who failed to abide by the divine rule book and so fell foul of the gods and were punished as a result. Two in particular seem extremely relevant to Western culture today: Midas and Narcissus.

The story of Midas and his Midas Touch is a well-known and charming myth (we touched on it in chapter 5), almost – and seemingly - harmless in its fairy story qualities. Luc Ferry[138] pointed out the story of Midas is often regarded as 'unimportant' and 'a fabliau without much import or significance'. But this fails to recognise its deeper truths.

In brief, the story runs that King Midas recognises the prisoner brought before him as Silenus, the rather ugly and dissipated god who was/is the step father of Dionysus[139]. Midas sees an opportunity: not only does he release him, he honours him by feasting and drinking in his honour for ten days and nights! When Dionysus learns of this, he is extremely grateful and offers Midas an incredible gift: namely, what would he like to have? This open-ended offer is immediately abused by Midas, who thus reveals his hubris. Without hesitation he replies, 'Pray grant that all I touch be turned into gold'.

And we all know what happens now: everything he touches does indeed become gold: everything! The myth, at this point, should perhaps remind us of Medusa, whom we also encountered in chapter 5. For in her case, her look turned living and organic matter to stone, literally petrifying it. Now we have the touch turning everything to gold. We note the extremes here: turning to stone is relatively a worthless ability, for stone is a cheap commodity, but turning to gold is not; gold is valuable, is precious. However, whether it be stone or gold is irrelevant, since both powers of transformation undermine life – and the living – itself.

And in the case of Midas, we have the folly of hubris – his request is out of all proportion to the benefit he had delivered to

---

[138] Luc Ferry, *The Wisdom of the Myths*, 2014.
[139] Dionysus, in Greek mythology, is the god of wine, revelry, theatre, fertility, and the life force. Known as Bacchus in Roman mythology, Dionysus is a complex and multifaceted deity whose myths and attributes reflect both joy and chaos.

Dionysus. It's as if (if we think about it) one had given somebody else's child a helpful lift home from school, and the grateful parent said, 'Thank you so much, what can I do for you?' and one replied, 'Buy me a 14-bedroom country mansion'. In a way, by being so generous to Silenus, Midas had set out to trick Dionysus into a generosity that he would exploit. But tricking a god is tricky, or to use Gollum's expression in the Lord of the Rings, 'tricksy', if not downright dangerous.

There is, then, hubris both in the request itself, which is out of all proportion to the actions of Midas in the first place – so incurs the censure of violating Apollo's maxim of the golden mean, or 'Not Too Much' – and it is hubristic in its essential nature, since like Medusa turning all to stone, we now have a human being who can turn all things to gold.

Fortunately, and perhaps because Midas is a true devotee of Dionysus (he fares much worse later when he crosses the god Apollo and is given ass's ears for his pains), and because Dionysus himself is a disrupter, this hubris is only lightly punished. When Midas discovers he can no longer eat or drink because everything he touches turns to gold, he pleads with Dionysus to remove the 'gift', which Dionysus does. Midas must go and wash in the river Pactolus, and there he is freed from the curse.

But what has this to do with the modern world and the West especially? Well, Bill Bonner[140] observed: "Try an experiment at home. Tell your teenager he will get $5,000 a month for the rest of his life, and a lifetime supply of marijuana. See how that stimulates him. Think he'll study harder, work harder?" The idea of having money for nothing, and something for nothing, and riches without any real effort on our part, are what is now endemic to our thought patterns – though one could hardly call it 'thinking'.

Post the 2008 financial crisis, and adding the Covid QE response along with it, some $9 trillion were added to the U.S. Federal Reserve; in the UK the figure is £895 billion[141]. This is an awful lot of money. A useful question might be: where is all this money coming from? And the technical answer might be: the Feds, or the Bank of England, or the governments etc. (Of course, more 'technical' still, the answer might be – the public through taxation!). The non-technical answer might be: it's all coming from the Midas Touch! 'We' are simply creating money – by fiat! 'Printing' money, as they say, or more accurately just digitising money into existence.

To be clear, nobody's performance has improved, there has been no increase in productivity – on the contrary, in the UK alone

---

[140] Bill Bonner, MoneyWeek, 5th April, 2019.
[141] https://www.federalreserve.gov/monetarypolicy/May-2022-Federal-Reserve-Balance-Sheet-Developments.htm?utm_source=chatgpt.com and https://commonslibrary.parliament.uk/research-briefings/sn02802/?utm_source=chatgpt.com

some 6% of GDP was lost in the 2008 crash and another 9.9% contraction during the Covid epidemic – and there has certainly been no uptick in most businesses' earnings, or profits (except in a few, celebrated and exceptional cases). It seems as if we are in a world where banks and governments can simply turn on the Midas Touch at will and print 'gold' – money that has not been earned in any meaningful way. As a sidebar here, we might add that the rise of Bitcoin is another form of unearned income: "Bitcoin has zero fundamental utility ... Its value ultimately depends on nothing more than the expectation a greater fool will pay more for it. It started life by posing as the great disruptor of regulated finance. Now absurdly the pitch is that people should buy it precisely because it is regulated by the SEC. How hard must the gods of finance be laughing?"[142]

Economists, of course, give contradictory advice about this situation. Some say, well, we did it in the financial crisis in 2008 and that saved the day and all turned out nice again; others argue that the circumstances in 2008 were fundamentally different to the circumstances today – for example, in 2008 the banks were under-capitalised and so could 'absorb' all the free money, which is not the case today – and so this is going to lead to a dreadful level of inflation that we have not experienced, since at least the 70's. Who's right?

Well, the answer is not to turn to economists, for what do they really know? As Warren Buffett acidly commented[143]: "Any company who has an economist has one employee is too many". No, the answer is in the Midas myth.

When we understand the myth, we see what it is telling us: that expecting something for nothing is not the way and always leads to disaster. It is hubris against the Greek gods and the structure of the cosmos; similar ideas occur in various religions and mythologies throughout the world, including the Chinese Tao Te Ching. So it is that Midas, with all the money in the world – all that gold – potentially ends up starving or thirsting to death. The creation of gold via magic leads to death. Imagine that! Here we are trying to save lives from a coronavirus, and yet we are potentially – through what we are doing – going to create a situation which destroys far more lives than we are saving!

And of course, what we haven't yet said is that not only is Midas stupid and hubristic, but one other aspect of these vices is augmented by his avarice: the wanting more and more at the expense of the common good. One of the remarkably bad things about the Covid-19 lockdown is not just the fact that the wealthy

---

[142] Bill Blaine on the Morning Porridge, cited Money Week 19th January 2024, by Alex Rankin, in New Bitcoin ETFs blow up a bubble.
[143] Cited MoneyWeek, Warren Buffett, 30th September, 2016.

have become significantly wealthier, but that ordinary people have been hoarding toilet paper, soap, and other types of hygiene products - their 'gold' as it were. Again, as Bill Bonner[144] puts it: 'A huge crisis - caused by fake money and fake thinking - is coming'.

But Midas doesn't die. In this case the god lets him off. But like Jesus telling the blind man to go and wash himself in the pool[145], Midas (who is also 'blind') too must wash himself. A kind of baptism, a dying to the old life, a healing and a being born anew? Can we do that? Can we turn from the avarice, the free money, and embrace a new way of living? Midas did. But then sadly, he went back to his old ways. It didn't end well for him, not well at all.

Pursuing, then, the double hubris of Midas: he had demanded an excessive gift from the god, Dionysus, and furthermore the gift itself destabilised the order of the cosmos, and so life itself. How could it not – his touch turning everything to gold? In one sense Midas's hubris is shown in his violation of Apollo's two maxims: first, Not Too Much, and clearly requesting this much gold clearly violated that injunction. And his second, which is Know Thyself. This latter injunction is often taken by the contemporary personal development movement as meaning: discover yourself, become more self-aware, and so grow as a person. The Greeks – and Apollo, however - didn't see it that way: for them, knowing yourself meant knowing your place in the scheme of the cosmos. That, you were mortal, not a god, and that, therefore, you submitted to their higher powers in all aspects of your life.

This idea is not unique to Greek classical thinking. The Ancient Egyptians refer to it[146]; the Old and New Testaments testify to the same thing; as does the Chinese I- Ching[147]: "They [the ancient peoples] put themselves in accord with the Tao and its power and in conformity with this laid down the order of what is right. By thinking through the order of the outer world to the end, and by exploring the law of their nature to the deepest core, they arrived at an understanding of fate." Here fate is what the gods ordain.

There is, then, a virtual universal witness to the concept of walking humbly with your God or gods, and to deviate from this path is to bring down punishment. Now in the case of Midas we saw that Dionysus was pretty lenient in terms of his treatment of Midas. Midas simply had to wash himself in a particular river and the gift – curse – was removed. Probably why the treatment was so lenient was to do with the fact that Midas was a true worshipper of

---

[144] Bill Bonner, MoneyWeek, 10th Jan 2020
[145] John's gospel, 9 v. 7
[146] The Book of the Dead.
[147] I-Ching

Dionysus and his cohort: it was perhaps to Dionysus a mildly amusing folly that Midas behaved as he did. But the thing is, Midas clearly learnt nothing from this experience, for the hubris and the folly accompany him to his next, and disastrous, exploit, which is almost as famous as his golden touch. Here he is to learn that hubris before the god Apollo has much graver consequences.

That Midas was a devout follower of Dionysus is shown in the fact that when he succeeded to the throne of Phrygia, Midas promoted the worship of Dionysus. It was onwards from this point that Midas witnessed the musical contest between Apollo and, some say Marsyas, and others, Pan, but the identity here is not so significant; for Marsyas was a satyr (who were male attendants of the god Dionysus, often naked, and known to be bestial and boisterous); Pan was the god of shepherds, flocks and fertility, or the 'goat-god'. Like Dionysus, then, both stand as antagonists in their antinomian and bestial aspects against all that Apollo represents.

Both challenged Apollo's musical supremacy, and a contest was arranged in which Tmolus, a river god, would be the umpire. Interestingly, Apollo would play his lyre, and Pan (and Marysas too) would play their pipes. Immediately, we see that we are talking about the contrast between the carefully controlled plucking of musical notes with mathematical precision versus the coarser charm of an instrument that one roughly blows into[148]. Taking the Pan version of the event, all who witnessed the playing of both musicians unanimously gave the verdict to Apollo: his music mesmerised them all.

All, that is, except Midas, who loudly and 'dissonantly' (a good word in this context) declared his preference for Pan's playing, claiming the verdict was 'unfair'! This act of incivility, this aesthetic lapse in taste, this predilection for the gross – this act of hubris before the god – could not be allowed to go unpunished. As Ovid writes it[149], "The god of Delos did not allow such undiscriminating ears to keep their human form, but drew them out and covered them with shaggy grey hair, and made them flexible at the base, and gave them powers of movement. Though the rest was human, he was punished in that sole aspect: he wore the ears of a slow-moving ass", and so Midas' ears are transformed into asses' ears to manifest his stupidity.

This is the beginning of the end for Midas, for it is as a direct result of this punishment and his attempts to conceal it that he ends up ordering the death of his own barber – a form of judicial murder – and subsequently, miserably killing himself by drinking bull's

---

[148] A sidebar here is that originally the goddess Athene played the pipes but when she saw how the blowing disfigured her face, she discarded the instrument.
[149] Ovid, Metamorphoses Book 11.

blood (note the bestial aspect yet again). But I think what is important about the story is its relevance for today.

It can be summed up in paraphrasing Plato's dictum[150]: "To love rightly is to love what is orderly and beautiful in an educated and disciplined way." And that is what art (in its widest sense) was and is, at least until the C20th; but now – alongside the political bestialities of communism and fascism – we have developed a taste for the brutish and the bestial in art too. More exactly, art reflects the falseness of the prevalent ideologies. For, put politely, as Tom Stoppard said[151], "Imagination without skill gives us modern art". Everywhere we look we find just such art, and nowhere better summed up than by Andy Warhol's candid comment: "Making money is art and working is art and good business is the best art". Wow! Who'd have thought that? We are almost back here to Midas' golden touch – that surely was art too! We think of the recent 'shredding' of Banksy's 'Girl with a Balloon', which, miraculously according to art 'experts', added 50% to its value, meaning it was now worth in excess of $2.4M[152].

To think like this is entirely Dionysian, and represents the gathering forces of chaos and disorder that undermine society and all right order. The opposite of this might be something like what the English artist, Stanley Spencer[153] noted: "One might never be able to conceive what Heaven is like, but nevertheless the contemplation of it is, I think, the greatest thing of all for the creative artist". Imagine that: our contemporary artists, musicians and poets 'contemplating heaven' as the source for their inspiration? What we are talking about here is the transcendent: some 'thing' bigger than humanity, or mankind, or humanist and secular utopias. Some 'thing' whereby we approach the deep truths of human nature and the human predicament.

Luc Ferry said[154], "Worth noting especially is that it is through music – the cosmic art above all others since it relies entirely upon a structure of sounds that must, so to speak, 'rhyme' or accord with one another – that the cosmos is saved." This is the high view, the high position, that is represented by Apollo and his art. Midas represents the corruption of taste, and so of values, which if the myth is to be believed – and I believe it – suggests that for all those mini-Midases of today it won't end well; for there are

---

[150] In dialogues such as the Symposium and the Phaedrus, Plato explores the concept of love (or eros) as an appreciation for beauty that leads the soul toward higher understanding and the contemplation of the Form of Beauty itself.
[151] Tom Stoppard, through his character Henry Carr, in his play Travesties, 1974.
[152] Subsequently, it was resold again for £18.5M: https://en.wikipedia.org/wiki/Love_is_in_the_Bin?utm_source=chatgpt.com
[153] Stanley Spencer made this statement in a letter he wrote to his friend Desmond Chute in 1932.
[154] Luc Ferry, *The Wisdom of the Myths*, 2014.

dark consequences for all those abandoning themselves to the Dionysian god. As Midas discovered for himself.

So much, then, for the perils of being and acting like a Midas – individually, or collectively. But what about Narcissus? Recently, Jordan B Peterson[155] described the Premier of Canada, Justin Trudeau, as a 'narcissist', and given the fact that he is a clinical psychologist, then one might legitimately think that he would know. The reasons why he did this we need not explore now, but the thing is: I have noticed increasingly in recent times that the accusation of 'narcissism' is being used against more and more people. Certainly, there are many famous people from the past who now merit that designation: Napoleon, Hitler, Henry VIII, and still more recently, Howard Hughes and even, up to the present, Kim Jong-un. So, to be in that company is not a good thing!

Of course, like any illness there is a spectrum: one can be mildly ill, chronically ill, acutely or even gravely ill. What, then, are the symptoms – as defined by modern psychiatry - of this condition? Here are some: Grandiosity (exaggeration of their achievements), need for admiration, lack of empathy, sense of entitlement, manipulative behaviour, fragile self-esteem, and difficulty in maintaining relationships. If you go on-line, you will find websites devoted to that most important topic of how you – you personally – can avoid getting entangled in a relationship with a 'narcissist'!

All this is very interesting, but more interesting still for me is: where does this concept of a narcissist come from and what else can we glean about narcissists if we consider the origins of the condition? As with virtually all Greek myths, there are always variants, but the essential story runs something like this: Narcissus was the beautiful son of the river god, Kephissos and the nymph, Liriope. With this god-infused parentage, his beauty was more or less guaranteed; and, indeed, he was astonishingly lovely so that by the time he was sixteen many young men and young women had hopelessly fallen in love with him. But he never reciprocated …

When Narcissus was still a baby his mother went to visit and ask the blind prophet, Tiresias, whether her son would live to a good old age. At the time, Tiresias was not well-known as the great seer and prophet he was to become, but his response to this enquiry was one of the reasons he subsequently became so famous. Tiresias replied: "Yes, so long as he never comes to know himself." This answer totally baffled the mother and the audience: 'Yes', but … what could the 'so long as…' mean? How does one come to 'know oneself'?

---

[155] Article in the UK's Daily Telegraph: https://www.telegraph.co.uk/news/2023/09/01/jordan-peterson-podcast-canada-decline-twitter-free-speech/

One of the rejected lovers of Narcissus was the nymph, Echo. She had been a busybody chattering to the queen of the gods, Hera, to distract her from noticing that Hera's husband, Zeus, king of the gods, was pursuing love affairs with other nymphs! As punishment, Hera cast a spell on her so that she could never speak except to repeat what somebody had said to her – an 'echo' if you will. But she fell in love with Narcissus, was rejected, and so pined away until her body was completely wasted and only her voice, her echo, remained.

At this point, having rejected so many, Nemesis[156] enters the story: for having rejected so many, Narcissus was made to 'feel' what it felt like to never be accepted by the one that you love. Exhausted from a day's hunting, and sitting down beside a pool to take a drink, he becomes spellbound with his own reflection in the pool: he sees his own image – so, 'knows himself' – but falls in love with that image. In fact, falls desperately in love with his own image, so much so that he cannot tear himself away from admiring it and yearning for it as the object of his love. Eventually, of course, he dies there.

As he was dying, he'd sigh and say things like, 'Alas' and 'in vain', and Echo would pick up these refrains and they would reverberate throughout the surrounding woodlands. It is said that even in Hades, the Underworld, that he kept looking at his reflection in the river Styx, the river the dead have to cross to literally depart from the land of the living. The obsession with himself, therefore, followed him beyond death. Back in the living world, he was transformed into the flower that bears his name.

So, what do we learn from this brief excursion into mythology? For me, perhaps the most important aspect of the story is the fact that (in the Apollonian sense), Narcissus doesn't really know himself at all: what he 'knows' is what he can tangibly see – his own image. And all of us have a self-image – a projection of who we want the world to think we are – but it is not 'us', it is not what we might call our true self, or using more ancient language, it is not our 'soul'. To the extent to which we become fully integrated and psychologically healthy human beings, the distance between what our self-image reveals and who we are in our souls is narrowed. Living in truth means how others perceive us is actually how we are. Nobody – with the exception of religious geniuses – manages to do that with much degree of precision.

But Apollo's injunction – to 'know thyself' – didn't just mean understand yourself psychologically; it has a specific spiritual sense: it meant know your limits. In other words, know the extent of your abilities, know your place in the social system, know that

---

[156] Or Artemis, the chaste huntress, or Aphrodite, goddess of love depending on your variant version.

you are mortal – and knowing you are mortal means, as a vital corollary, that you must know that the gods are above and they are NOT mortal: we owe them worship and obedience. Indeed, the most heinous crimes in ancient Greek thought were crimes of hubris: where gods were mocked or explicitly disobeyed. It was Plato, much later, who redefined 'know thyself' as meaning understand your own soul, your own psychology.

Either way, though, whether we consider Narcissus as someone who did not know himself in the sense that he did not understand his limits – and so transgressed the divine order and through hubris effectively worshipped himself – or as someone who could only see superficially – and so not understand his soul – and thus became totally dominated by 'surfaces', the material, and the obvious; or to put the 'material and the obvious' another way: by the non-spiritual; either way we find someone who is doomed to grief and an ultimate despair: for they can never have what they so desperately yearn for, since what they yearn for is beyond the limits of human possibilities.

A secondary point, however, relates to Apollo's second maxim: 'Not too much' (or, avoid extremes!). When we look at Narcissus clearly, we see that he was completely preoccupied (to the exclusion of everyone else) with himself; but interestingly, we see exactly the reverse with Echo – she is completely besotted with someone else, Narcissus, at the expense of her own existence; she becomes an 'echo', a mere shadow of a personality, indeed of reality itself. Thus, in a yin and yang kind of way, we see a contrasting lack of balance in these two mythological figures. Combined, perhaps, they could have made one healthy, wholesome individual, but that was never to be and never could be.

Earlier, I talked about seven symptoms of clinical narcissism, and they are bad enough: just take the first symptom, grandiosity. Who likes anyone who exaggerates their accomplishments and trades on their 'doing' rather than their 'being' human? No-one, except possibly the greatly deceived and deceivers themselves. But here's the point: I mentioned the increasing use of the term 'narcissist' to describe anyone's or any party's enemy. There seems to be a lot of it about and I am not surprised. For, think about it: what are all these hydra-headed utopian groups, projects, Woke virtue-signalling activities with which we are beset, other than profound forms of narcissism?

Why? Because all desperately yearn to do what I have outlined above as being to go 'beyond the limits of human possibilities': to make people 'equal' – as if that could ever be the case; to annul sexual differentiation – as if nature had no say in the matter; to stop the temperature of the Earth rising – as if this were solely a human choice; and so on. Being a narcissist is a profound and debilitating condition, and the terrifying thing is that more and more people seem to be cursed with it: they were born beautiful (like Narcissus) but in their overweening pride Nemesis has cut them down – for, in time, like Narcissus himself, they will fail, just as their true 'love' will never materialise. So – meanwhile - watch them bibble-babbling still as they are forced to cross the river Styx!

Chapter 8:
Truth and her Twin: Mendacium

We have looked at a heroic descent into Hell by Orpheus, and then considered a couple of dodgy characters (although of noble descent) called Midas and Narcissus; and these last two begin to remind us very strongly of the kind of people who live with us today: obsessed with wealth (gold) and obsessed with appearances (reflections and images). In short, a world where our real life – the life of the soul - is swamped with greed and with self-obsession. There is good, it seems, and there is evil; two sides of a coin, twins even, though very different. Truth and falsehood: the gods enjoin us to be good, to join the heroic quest of conquering evil, smiting falsehood, but all too often we turn away from this destiny and choose – not a destiny – but a fate that condemns us.

But the idea of twins has always been a fascination. For example, although the Bible doesn't explicitly say so, Cain and Abel are often regarded as twins; and even if they weren't, Esau and Jacob, a bit later on in the Genesis narrative, definitely were; and interestingly, as it also says in the Bible[157] God loved Jacob, but Esau He hated. There is so often a chalk-and-cheese aspect to twins: despite clearly being similar, their fates are very different.

We see this even in something like the founding of Rome: Romulus, the twin of Remus, gets all the credit (the name Rome gives that away) and finally gets taken to heaven by his father Mars/Ares, although he has slain his twin brother (as Cain slew his brother Abel).

Not all twin stories showed differentiation through moral virtue or turpitude, but profound division there invariably is. Pollux loved his twin brother Castor, but they too were chalk-and-cheese in that Pollux was immortal whereas Castor was not. Eventually, 'twin-ness' was immortalised by them for us in the constellation we call Gemini.

Why are we so fascinated by twins? I think for two primary reasons. In our own time they have become an inexhaustible source of inquiry for helping scientists trying to establish whether it is nature or nurture that determines who we are and what we do. If two people have near identical genetic codes, so the reasoning goes, then in separating them at birth, we should be able to see how much genetics plays its part in their individual destinies, versus the nurturing they have received.

But perhaps there is a more important subconscious reason: Namely, they represent to us in visual form the issue of appearance

---

[157] Malachi 1. v. 2-3

and reality. We have this insatiable hunger to know whether what we are seeing—the appearance—is real, is true, or whether it is not.

This question is true philosophically: We have all probably heard of the Buddhist aphorism about the man dreaming he was a butterfly, but on waking up wondered whether he was now a butterfly dreaming he was a man! Be that as it may, the importance of whether something is an appearance or a reality is nowhere more critical for us than in our dealings with other people.

Our whole human history and all our important literature concerns this question. Shakespeare explored this comically in his "The Comedy Errors", which hinges on two sets of twins being mistaken for each other! And this plot device Shakespeare liked so much he was to use it again; for example, in "Twelfth Night" where the twins are actually a brother and sister, and yet nevertheless are able to pass off for one another. I think what we are really talking about here is the question of truth.

Aesop tells a fable[158] that explains how this came about. Prometheus created human beings, and had always been their great friend. The name Prometheus means 'forethought' – although a Titan, he was a god of wisdom because he could see ahead; it was this seeing that enabled him personally to avoid the fate of the other Titans, condemned to Tartarus by Zeus, since he foresaw that Zeus would win and joined his side.

Prometheus created human beings and was very pro-human beings; so much so that eventually, in disobeying Zeus and giving mankind fire, he suffered an eternal punishment (though was freed from it by the hero, Herakles). But before all that occurred, Prometheus decided to help mankind further by enabling them to communicate and behave better. To this end he decided to sculpt a new form called Veritas[159] or Truth; and if Truth came alive, then this would help people in their interactions and behaviour. But as he was working on this project – he was a potter – he was summoned by almighty Zeus and so had to leave his workshop.

Because he had recently acquired an apprentice, Dolus (Deception), Prometheus left him in charge of his workshop. In the brief time that Prometheus was away, Dolus, who was ambitious, had accessed the clay and fashioned a virtually identical figure to the Truth that Prometheus had created. The only difference was that the copy did not have feet as Dolus had run out of clay. When Prometheus returned, Dolus retired in fear, but Prometheus was amazed at the similarity of the two statues and – sadly - wanted to take credit for both. So, both models went into the kiln, were baked, and became infused with life.

Thus, a new pair of twins was born: One, Veritas or Truth

---

[158] https://www.theoi.com/Daimon/Pseudologoi.html
[159] The word lives in English still: verily, verily – truly, truly, and also in the word veritable

walked with steady, measured steps; and second, her twin, Mendacium (or Falsehood), who because she had no feet, could hardly stand and certainly could not move. Aesop concluded, therefore, that although Falsehood might appear to be successful, at least initially, its footless limitation meant inevitably that Truth would prevail against it.

Nice thought. If that only seemed true today. As Michel de Montaigne[160] observed, "If falsehood, like truth, had only one face, we would be in better shape. For we would take as certain the opposite of what the liar said. But the reverse of truth has a hundred thousand shapes and a limitless field." We are ever more, it seems, waging war – in the media, in social media, in the hearts and minds of the population – against falsehood, against 'fake news', against misrepresentation at the deepest levels of mendacity, against the twin Mendacium, which seems so similar to Veritas. However, victory is not easy and does not seem a foregone conclusion. But it is vitally important that we continue to strive for Truth, for as Dr. Johnson[161] said, "The mind can only repose upon the stability of truth," which requires feet, stability, in other words! Without Truth, we are "footless"; we cannot go anywhere and of course we are not rooted, as in that Tai Chi sense of being rooted firmly to the ground, so that our balance is secure. We are in short unbalanced, easy to tip over, unstable.

To recover Veritas, therefore, we need to examine 'things' closely, very closely indeed, so that we can spot the difference: Which is Veritas, and which is the idol that seems identical but has no feet?

If we think through what this imagery means – keeping in mind that the myths tell us deep psychological or even spiritual truths – we realise that being footless, being immobile, means that we are not free. The essence of being free is that we are free to move, wherever and whenever we want. If at any point in our lives we cannot move, we cannot truly be said to be free.

At a religious level, for example, Christ talked about knowing the truth and the truth setting us free[162] and this, as it were, philosophical idea was matched by his healing of the physically infirm – some of whom could not even move – and by the healing, not just curing their bodies, but setting them free to stand, to move. Truth has this remarkable quality: it frees us. But equally, not just at a religious level, but at a political one too. If we cannot move – for example, as in a lockdown (think Covid), a curfew, embargo and so on – then we are not free politically. Not to

---

[160] Sherlock Holmes, cited MoneyWeek 24th June 2016; however more likely to be from Michel de Montaigne, *Essays*. reflects on the complexity of falsehood and truth in his essay "Of Liars."
[161] Dr Johnson, Samuel Johnson's *The Rambler*, essay No. 7, published on April 10, 1750
[162] John 8. V2

be misunderstood: there may be good reasons – public health etc. – for a lockdown, but nevertheless, the imposition of one creates a lack of freedom.

This issue, then, is really important. In a way what I am saying is that the acceptance of Mendacium – Lies or Error – is the precursor to a loss of freedom. It is not necessarily immediately apparent that we have lost our freedom, but if enough people collectively subscribe to Mendacium, then as sure as night follows day, our freedoms are eroded and we become enslaved by false and lying ideologies.

We are today being assaulted on all sides by just such a lying ideology, a Mendacium threatening to undermine all our freedoms. In terms of identifying it, Theodore Dalrymple[163] perhaps caught its very essence when he wrote: "He [Stefan Zweig] would have viewed with horror the cacophony of monomanias - sexual, racial, social, egalitarian - that marks the intellectual life of our societies, each monomaniac demanding legislative restriction on the freedom of others in the name of a supposed greater, collective good." Notice the strength of feeling in that statement: not people, but monomaniacs, demanding what? Our freedom for some 'supposed greater, collective good.'

And less we think that the danger can only come from self-evident monomaniacs (and self-confessed communists) – as visible as some of them are, aggressively protesting on our streets – yet the danger of Mendacium can be much subtler. It can be a lie generated by an internal contradiction which is difficult to spot. Take, for example, Camille Paglia's comment[164] on modern liberalism and its connection to feminism: "Modern liberalism suffers unresolved contradictions. It exalts individualism and freedom and, on its radical wing, condemns social orders as oppressive. On the other hand, it expects the government to provide materially for all, a feat manageable only by an expansion of authority and a swollen bureaucracy... In other words, liberalism defines the government as a tyrant father but demands that it behaves as nurturant mother... Feminism has exceeded its proper mission of seeking political equality for women and has ended by rejecting contingency, that is, human limitation by nature or fate."

Isn't this the essence of Mendacium? So close to Veritas. Surely, we can all agree that it is right that women should be treated equally with men, but along the way this 'truth' has morphed – via Modern Liberalism - into a lie: a lie that denies 'human limitation', which is the actual difference between men and women, or their nature; and also, has denied 'fate'. We may wish to have another word for this – destiny, providence, the Tao. But whatever word we

---

[163] Theodore Dalrymple, *Our Culture, What's Left of It*, 2005,
[164] Camille Paglia, *Sexual Personae*, 1992,

have, we'd realise if we understood it, that outcomes in life never have been, never will be, 'equal'. That striving for equality of outcomes is utopian, futile and ultimately 'anti-freedom'; for what does it mean to be free? It means we take self-responsibility, and as a consequence we each achieve different results for ourselves. On an individual level this is obviously true, but we have seen in history plenty of collective efforts to reverse this situation. And, as Jordan B. Peterson[165] put it, "If there was any excuse to be a Marxist in 1917, there is absolutely and finally no excuse now."

This encroachment of Mendacium on the domain of Veritas often seems to start with small things. In the UK, for example, Robert Oulds in his book, Moralitis[166], comments on Student Unions which "ensure freedom from speech through 'no-platforming' and 'safe spaces'". Notice the rather witty, 'freedom from speech', not 'of speech. It almost seems funny until one reflects that we are talking about the young university generation whom we once thought went – like those of us before – to university to broaden and expand their minds. Weren't universities places that had famous debating chambers? No more it seems – the poor 'snowflakes' cannot abide an idea that contradicts their uninformed prejudices[167]. Worse, this is like an insidious cancer which spreads so that soon the whole body is riddled with it. Quoting Dalrymple again, we end up with, "a society of "emasculated liars" who are very easy to control[168]."

How do we resist this insidious undermining of all that we hold dear? Clearly, there is no easy answer, for if there were, we wouldn't have the problem. But I make two suggestions that seem relevant.

One, is honest journalism of the type that GB News in the UK, and say, The Epoch Times in the USA, espouses: There has to be resistance to the fake news and social media control that currently now appears. In a way, this is immediate and frontline stuff. We can spot that these outlets are espousing actual news because of the hostility they attract from Left-wing commentators. We need to do all we can to promote them and to not promote organisations such as the Guardian and the BBC. The BBC license fee is well-overdue for scrapping – why do British people have to subsidise a news organisation that does not provide them with real news?

But the deeper, longer-term stuff is related to the kind of culture we live in and the values it promotes and may sometimes

---

[165] Jordan B. Peterson, cited MoneyWeek 16th November, 2018.
[166] Robert Oulds and Neil McCrae, *Moralitis: A Cultural Virus*, 2020.
[167] Durham University, as this is being written, is involved in a spat in which the 200-year-old Durham Union is being banned by the University's own militant Student Union.
[168] Robin Aitken's book, *The Noble Liar*, 2018, makes a persuasive case for seeing the whole BBC as a news distortion outlet rather than a true purveyor of news stories.

seem to contradict. In particular, I feel that our arts are of primary importance in this battle for the hearts and souls of the people, but especially the younger generation. Why is this? Because it is the arts – literature, drama, music and visual art – that most affects our emotions. In the absence of any pervasive spiritual or religious tradition, our sense of the creative can only derive from these sources.

The trouble is, so much 'art' today is either entirely nihilistic or not-art at all! John Hapgood[169] (former Archbishop of York) some while ago observed, "The fact that not much art these days seems to be inspired by explicitly religious themes may, however, be a reflection of the trivialisation and disorientation of art itself."

The problem is: people no longer believe in anything, including 'form' itself – hence, in poetry, 'free verse', meaning, usually, poetry with no structure at all, and so very little beauty – or truth. What is true of today's poetry is also true of the other art forms – we all know it but, as with the Emperor's new clothes, like to pretend otherwise.

Thus, we need to press for art that rediscovers the myths of old, but for a contemporary generation. The great critic Northrop Frye [170]said, "A myth is designed not to describe a specific situation but to contain it in a way that does not restrict its significance to that one situation. Its truth is inside its structure, not outside." This is the real twin, Veritas, which compels assent because its truth is inside, is internal, and this is the only one that can really stand.

We come full circle then: for the essence of Truth is that it stands; the nature of Mendacium is that it falls; and the circle is this – to stand means wholeness, completeness, order, whereas to fall means to break, fragment, collapse, and to enter into disorder. All that Zeus stood for in creating the cosmos and rendering it habitable becomes undone once we start accepting the falsehood as being the real thing. Every lie – every piece of fake news – every gross or selective misrepresentation – that is put out on media and on social media, and which is also exchanged between individuals – contributes to disorder and breakdown, and so leads to chaos. Ultimately, in human terms, this results in the Four Horsemen of the Apocalypse[171]: conquest, famine, war and death!

To recap then: the mythological theme of twins, as we've seen, consistently invokes the idea of duality: opposing forces, complementary yet antagonistic. It's no wonder that in many

---

[169] John Hapgood, Varieties of Unbelief, 2000.
[170] Northrop Frye, *The Great Code*. 1982.
[171] Revelation 6:1-8: the White, Red, Black and Pale Horses. Of particular interest and relevance here is the Black horse of famine: This rider carries a pair of scales, symbolizing famine. The black horse is often seen as representing scarcity and economic hardship, where essential goods become exceedingly costly. The text refers to food rationing and a warning against harming luxuries like oil and wine, suggesting a contrast between poverty for some and continued wealth for others.

ancient cultures, twins were regarded with both awe and trepidation, as they were seen as manifestations of cosmic balance—forces of light and dark, good and evil, or life and death. This duality is central not only in mythology but also in the way we perceive the world today, as our modern issues of truth versus falsehood show.

It's intriguing to consider that this division, this twinship, extends not only to the grandiose myths and the cosmos but also to the very nature of human experience. In ancient mythology, these distinctions were often simplified to a moral binary: heroes fought to preserve order (cosmos) against chaos (often represented by monsters, deceit, or nature itself). But today, we face an overwhelming multiplicity of narratives, each claiming to hold the mantle of truth. This proliferation of perspectives, while perhaps a reflection of the complexity of the modern world, creates a landscape where distinguishing Veritas from Mendacium becomes ever more difficult.

A prime example of this can be found in our digital age, where the spread of information, and equally disinformation, has become virtually unchecked. What once required the steady movement of Veritas—the slow but inevitable triumph of truth—has now become a battle in which Mendacium, through the immediacy of technology, has an unprecedented advantage. While Aesop's fable emphasizes that falsehood lacks the foundation to stand the test of time, we are increasingly seeing that in a world where immediacy is often mistaken for validity, Mendacium can gain a foothold, however temporary, that it never could before.

Here we find ourselves at a critical juncture. Much like the mythological twins, there is a struggle between two very different approaches to reality. On one hand, we have the slower, often laborious, journey to uncover Veritas. On the other, we have the seductive allure of Mendacium, dressed in a garb so similar to truth that, at a glance, it can deceive even the most discerning observer. It's as though, in our age, Mendacium has gained the ability to sprout feet—or at least the appearance of them—through the medium of instantaneous communication.

As technology advances, the gap between appearance and reality grows ever wider. Social media, for instance, creates curated realities—images and personas designed to project an ideal, often far removed from the truth. This is not unlike the myth of Narcissus (whom we saw earlier), who fell in love with his reflection, mistaking appearance for reality. Our own digital reflections—Instagram filters, manipulated photos, AI, selectively shared posts—are increasingly blurring the lines between what is real and what is fabricated. Narcissus, captivated by his own image, could not tear himself away, and in doing so, he perished. Are we not, in many ways, modern Narcissuses, caught in the reflection of our digital selves?

This brings us to the heart of the matter: freedom. As discussed earlier, Veritas sets us free. But how can we be free when we are trapped in the maze of Mendacium? In mythology, the heroes' quest is always a journey towards truth and freedom—whether it's Orpheus descending into the underworld to retrieve his beloved or Prometheus defying the gods to bring fire (symbolic of knowledge and truth) to humanity. These myths underscore the importance of truth in achieving not just physical freedom, but spiritual and intellectual freedom.

But what of today's heroes? Who is standing up to the forces of Mendacium? It seems the battle has shifted from the individual hero's quest to a collective struggle, one in which society as a whole must participate. This is a battle not fought with swords and shields but with critical thinking, discernment, and a willingness to question the narratives we are fed. Yet, it is becoming increasingly difficult to be a hero in a world that rewards the swift spread of lies over the slow uncovering of truth.

The philosopher Hannah Arendt[172] spoke of the "banality of evil," the idea that great harm is often done not by villains with grandiose schemes but by ordinary people who fail to question the systems of falsehood they are a part of. In much the same way, Mendacium gains power not through its inherent strength but through the passive acceptance of its existence. When lies become so ubiquitous that they are seen as the norm, society begins to lose its ability to recognize Veritas, and with that, it loses its freedom.

Consider, too, the psychological toll of living in a world where truth is constantly under siege. There is a growing sense of disillusionment and apathy, a resignation to the idea that truth may never prevail, or worse, that it no longer matters. This is perhaps the greatest victory of Mendacium—not that it can defeat Veritas in a direct confrontation, but that it can erode the will to seek truth at all. In this way, Mendacium's lack of feet becomes irrelevant, for if no one is looking for Veritas, then what need is there for movement?

However, we must remember that mythology is, at its core, a guide for living. These stories are not relics of a bygone era but timeless teachings that resonate with the human condition. In the myth of Prometheus, we are reminded that even the gods can be challenged when the cause is just. The fire that Prometheus steals from the gods to give to mankind is a form of truth – and with it comes great responsibility, and it is up to us to nurture it, protect it, and, when necessary, fight for it.

---

[172] Hannah Arendt, *Eichmann in Jerusalem: A Report on the Banality of Evil* (1963).

So, how do we reclaim Veritas in a world dominated by Mendacium? It begins with a conscious effort to engage with the world critically, to question what we are told, and to seek out the deeper truths that lie beneath the surface. It requires us to reject the easy allure of superficial answers (and a great example of that are internet memes) and to embrace the complexity of reality. Just as the mythological heroes had to face trials and tribulations in their quest for truth, so too must we be willing to confront the uncomfortable truths of our time.

In conclusion, the battle between Veritas and Mendacium is not just a mythological concept but a living reality that we face every day. It is a struggle that requires vigilance, courage, and an unwavering commitment to truth. And while Mendacium may seem to have the upper hand in the short term, we must take solace in the fact that, like in Aesop's fable, truth has the feet to carry it forward, while falsehood is ultimately immobile, doomed to collapse under the weight of its own contradictions.

Chapter 9:
Apollo, Mnemosyne, and Poetry

Our last chapter discussed the imperative for distinguishing between Truth (Veritas) and Falsehood (Mendacium), and how in our modern, digital era this is becoming increasingly difficult. Also, we talked about a shift from the individual hero to the more collective effort to resist falsehood; falsehood, which is also, of course, another name for evil. For to spell it out again, and to use the metaphor that we had in the original myth, falsehood has no feet, and so falls over; which is another way of saying, it generates disorder – to use Yeats' expression[173], '… things fall apart; the centre cannot hold…' It acts against the very cohesion of the cosmos; it defies Zeus.

It is because this is so that we need to return to a god whom we have already encountered in chapter 2: Apollo. Apollo is the god par excellence whose maxims advocate civility, restraint, moderation, order and … truth. Why? Well, for one thing Apollo is the god of the sun, and so god of light; and light is always not only physical light in ancient texts, but the light of illumination – of knowledge and insight and prophecy: an understanding of the deep things of the dark where light probes, penetrates, and prevails.

It should be no surprise to learn, then, that not only is Apollo god of light, but he is also god of healing – light that heals and enables growth - and god of poetry and the arts. And this is important for our discussion in the last chapter: how do we overcome Mendacium or falsehood? Clearly, there is no easy answer, but one strand towards an answer is understanding the importance of the arts, but in particular of poetry in our culture generally and in our education system specifically. Poetry – and alongside it, myth – is one massive antidote to Mendacium.

Before looking at this in more detail, what exactly is the relationship between Apollo and poetry? Apollo, in Greek mythology, is deeply connected with poetry as he is regarded as the god of music, poetry, and the arts, among other things. His association with poetry primarily comes from his role as a patron of the Muses, who are the goddesses of artistic inspiration, including epic poetry, lyric poetry, and music. Apollo was often depicted with a lyre, symbolizing his influence over both music and the harmonious nature of poetic expression.

There are several layers to Apollo's connection with poetry. First, is the generally accepted fact that he was the leader (and patron) of the Muses. Who were the Muses? These were the

---

[173] W.B. Yeats. His poem, The Second Coming.

immortal beings – nine of them – who inspired artists, poets, musicians in nine areas of the artistic domains: The nine Muses are:

1. Calliope – Muse of epic poetry.
2. Clio – Muse of history.
3. Erato – Muse of love poetry.
4. Euterpe – Muse of music and lyric poetry.
5. Melpomene – Muse of tragedy.
6. Polyhymnia – Muse of sacred hymns and poetry.
7. Terpsichore – Muse of dance.
8. Thalia – Muse of comedy.
9. Urania – Muse of astronomy.

Calliope, muse of epic poetry (considered the greatest[174] of the nine domains) is the leader within the Nine, but Apollo is the leader of the Nine. It is instructive to reflect on the origins of the Muses: they were begotten in the nine nights of love-making between Zeus and Mnemosyne, the Titaness of memory.

Two things need comment here: first, memory is involved in all artistic acts. We cannot forget the past. As GK Chesterton[175] noted, "The boldest plans for the future invoke the authority of the past." The stupidest - and modernist - idea (expressed in Ezra Pound's dictum[176]: "Make it new") is that we can erase the past and build everything new and shining and perfect from scratch; this really is an idea for the birds, as well as being an aspect of that general drive for utopia that infects all minds that accept it. But just as important is the notion that the Muses were begotten: in other words, through sexual acts. That there were nine nights of love-making indicates the level of arousal and passion that Zeus and Memory experienced towards each other! So not a one-night stand then. Keep in mind here, too, that the coupling of Zeus with the Titaness (remember the Titans from Chapter 1?) is the joining of the old order with the new so that a yet more 'new' order can be produced – and critically, one that displays more beauty.

If all that weren't enough, Apollo's interest in poetry is extensive: Apollo's instrument is the lyre, which is not just a symbol of music but also of lyric poetry, which in ancient Greece was often sung to musical accompaniment. Poets and bards looked to Apollo for inspiration in creating works that were melodious and expressive. Further, at the Oracle of Delphi, as the god of prophecy and the sun, Apollo had an association with truth and

---

[174] Though Aristotle in his Poetics puts Tragedy on a par with Epic.
[175] G.K. Chesterton, "The Antiquity of Civilization," The Everlasting Man.
[176] Ezra Pound: The phrase has been traced to a passage in The Cantos, his long, complex, unreadable modernist poem. Specifically, in Canto 53, Pound describes an anecdote about the Chinese Emperor Tching Tang, who is said to have inscribed the phrase "Make it new" on his bath tub as a kind of daily motto.

enlightenment, central themes in poetic expression. Poets often sought to reveal truths about human nature and the world, much as Apollo's oracle would reveal divine truths. This aspect also aligns with poetry's power to convey wisdom, vision, and insight, drawing a parallel between the clarity of prophecy and the clarity poetry can bring to complex emotions and ideas. Apollo was also the patron of poetic competitions in ancient Greece, most notably at the Pythian Games, held in his honour at Delphi. These contests included not just athletic competitions but also artistic events, where poets, musicians, and performers would compete for Apollo's favour.

Finally, as we've already intimated, Apollo is often seen as the leader of the Muses, who are the goddesses of different artistic domains, including poetry. The relationship between Apollo and the Muses underscores his role as the god who inspires poets and artists, guiding them to create works of beauty, harmony, and truth. In essence, Apollo's connection to poetry is deeply intertwined with his broader role as a god of arts, prophecy, and enlightenment, highlighting poetry's power to both inspire and communicate deeper truths.

So, 'inspire and communicate deeper truths' – the opposite of Mendacium. Let's look at this issue, then, in a little more detail. And first, consider what literature – and poetry particularly – should be. To understand that, we need to use traditional writings naturally! To keep it simple, I would say that poetry has to represent the good, the true and most importantly of all, the beautiful. Philosophical and religious texts can be good and true, but it is the special quality of literature – of poetry – to be beautiful. The reason for the beauty is, of course, form: form is where we have structure and order, and this impresses itself upon our senses.

However, it is important to deflate one implication of this which the modern mind just loves to deduce and mock: namely, that wanting 'beauty' means wanting the saccharine, the bland and the non-challenging types of writing; a kind of literature that is the equivalent to an old-fashioned Disney film – no sex, no 'real' violence, and no 'issues' that might tax us; in other words, sugary versions of pure nostalgia and escapism. But any consideration of, say, the great traditional and even sacred (for example, The Psalms) texts such as Homer or Dante or Shakespeare would utterly refute this. But unlike modern and postmodern texts, which simply revel in sex, violence, horror, perversion and revulsion for their own sakes - and for the sake of being 'real' and 'realistic' - the 'classics' frame these things so that they are – despite the horrors of life, especially modern life - still 'good, true, and beautiful.'

Homer is full of violence, but it is profound and true to human nature; and alongside it go other qualities, such as when at last the anger of Achilles is satisfied, and with his enemy, king

Priam, both men mourn together and suffer their respective losses. Through this their common and shared humanity is established. Dante explores sex, violence and revulsion and more besides, but always in the context of the first line of his poem[177]: Nel mezzo del cammin di nostra vita – 'in the middle of OUR life', not just his. We are journeying to heaven with him, and this provides an overarching meaning to all the troubles we experience on Earth. And as for Shakespeare, where to begin? So many works – but who matches Macbeth in ambition, treachery and violence? How deep, though, the depiction of all this; and how inevitable its outcome, demonstrating – though with some degree of ambiguity which, for example, Polanski's film version evinces[178] – goodness in its triumph over evil. One genius aspect of this triumph is of course the fact of how evil defeats itself, although seemingly invincible.

Now this is all very well, but why should we have such great classics on our school and university curricula? What does goodness, truth and beauty mean in that context? Aren't these words just abstractions? They are, but their substance seems to me entirely practical, for it leads me to conclude that a study of the great classics – inspired by Apollo[179] - provides us with three overarching benefits. These are:

1. Role models of greatness
2. Deeper understandings of ourselves and others
3. Appreciation of form – hence beauty

Let's briefly consider each of these three Apollonian benefits.

First, role models of greatness. It says in the Bible[180] that "without vision the people perish". This applies to all levels of society: at a family level, community level, with our schools and colleges, with our institutions and businesses, and at government level. We have all experienced that sickening sense of drift and chaos that occurs where there is no vision; and where does vision come from? Great men and great women who galvanise those around them. But where does their vision come from? From role models of greatness: either in real life – for example, a great mother, a great father, a great teacher and so on – or from great books and great literature.

---

[177] Dante, *The Divine Comedy*, Inferno, Canto 1.
[178] In Polanski's film version the ambiguity of the ending comes from the fact that Fleance, son of Banquo, is seen as alive and subtly threatening to the new reign of Malcolm that has been established.
[179] Quite literally so in the case of Dante: "O good Apollo, for this last task make me as one of your own vessels, as you, from the laurel tree, demanded, to gain the highest prize." Paradiso, Canto 1: lines 13-21, Allen Mandelbaum translation.
[180] Proverbs 29 v18

It would be blindingly too obvious to cite all the great men and women whom the Bible has inspired to provide vision to their contemporaries – there are so many. But take Mother Teresa or take Martin Luther King – they were great, they had a vision, and they were inspired by what they read in the Bible.

In the same way, others have been inspired by poetry: Alexander was inspired by Homer. Almost the greatest miracle that Alexander[181] could conceive of was that Homer might return from the dead; and he based his whole life on imitating Achilles, the great Homeric hero. You might say, 'But that's not great – Alexander was not a man of peace.' But that is us imposing our values on him: at the time, everyone knew that he was great, they named him 'the Great', and for all that, with all the evil in him (Dante assigned him to a river of blood in Canto 12 of his Inferno), he had certain qualities we all can admire: his courage was simply legendary. Like Achilles - his hero - he was fearless. Courage is timeless – and in poetry we can experience it perfected.

But if that seems a step too far: take Winston Churchill, the great British war leader in World War II. His great role model was his own ancestor[182], John Marlborough, Duke of Blenheim, who won the Battle of Blenheim (1704) in the early Eighteenth century, and so prevented the European continent being dominated by France for a century (till the rise of Napoleon). So far so historical. But who inspired Marlborough? Marlborough claimed that Shakespeare was essential to his education and ideas – they inspired him, especially the History plays. But who inspired Shakespeare? Step forward the great Roman writer Plutarch. And if at this suggestion you want to say, Plutarch isn't a poet, but an historian, keep in mind the Nine Muses we mentioned earlier, including astronomy, comedy, dance, eloquence, epic, history, music, amatory poetry, and tragedy. Homer was epic (Calliope); Plutarch history (Clio)!

Finally, on the topic of role models: this is not something just about the noteworthies of yesteryear. Watch young people wanting to be Harry Potter; watch old and young adults at Star Wars conventions identifying with their heroes. Part of our self-concept is the 'ideal self' – the person we aspire to be. Literature gives us great models we can emulate; and poetry gives us the very greatest models (aside from religious personages). The corollary of this is: if the literature does not promote goodness, truth and beauty, what does it encourage? And the answer is obvious: corruption, mendacity and ugliness. Does that sound familiar?

---

[181] What can you tell me that deserves such excitement, except perhaps that Homer has come back to life? – Alexander the Great reportedly said. Plutarch and Robin Lane Fox
[182] Cited, Allan Bloom, *The Closing of the American Mind*.

Does that sound a lot like modern art and poetry? As Allan Bloom[183] expressed it, "Failure of culture is now culture."

The second wonder of studying and reading the great classics is the way it enables us to understand ourselves more deeply, as well as others. This should be clear anyway from what we have already said about Marlborough learning from Shakespeare who learnt from Plutarch. But what did he learn? Essentially, he learnt about statesmanship (because that interested him; others, of course, will learn other things). What is statesmanship? It is about conducting the business of a government and shaping its policies whilst being a wise, skilful, and respected political leader. If that doesn't require a profound understanding of human nature – of self and of others – it's difficult to imagine what would count!

Furthermore, to understand ourselves we need to remember GK Chesterton's admonishment[184]: "Every man has forgotten who he is. One may understand the cosmos, but never the ego; the self is more distant than any star." Perseus cannot face his greatest fear (none of us can!). Who/What is his greatest fear? Why, Medusa, the Gorgon, of course! But the goddess Athene, the goddess of wisdom, instructs him how he can face her: by using his polished shield as a mirror – we approach reality through reflection. In literary terms, we approach it through metaphor (which is why Aristotle said the mastery of metaphor was a sign of genius); and so metaphor – poetry - is for approaching our self that we have forgotten and cannot find because, as St Francis of Assisi allegedly[185] observed: "What you are looking for is what is looking". The eye – the I – which sees everything, cannot see itself, except by reflection. Thus, literature, poetry and theatre especially, provides us with just that reflection: we get to 'see' ourselves as we truly are.

Finally, in this all too brief overview, the appreciation of form. The deployment of form(s) and its appreciation is on the one hand a skill and knowledge set. Shakespeare writes blank verse; we not only see it on the page, but we hear it on stage or in our minds as we read. But on the other hand, it is much more than that. Dante's The Divine Comedy is possibly, in the non-religious domain, the greatest and most successfully structured poem ever written: the numerology involved in the 100 cantos is astonishing, but then so is, at the micro-level, the actual form of terza rima itself: 3-line stanzas representing a profound tribute to the triune God whom we will encounter in the final canto of the sequence: the rhyming scheme of the poem, simply awesome in its power,

---

[183] Allan Bloom, ibid.
[184] Cited, A Theology of Wonder, Brian P Gillen.
[185] The quote "What you are looking for is what is looking" is often attributed to St. Francis of Assisi, but there is no evidence in his writings or historical accounts that he actually said or wrote it. The saying aligns more closely with mystical and contemplative traditions, possibly influenced by later spiritual thinkers or translators interpreting his ideas.

complexity and sustained brilliance and beauty. Short lyricists may be compared to 100 or even 800-meter runners; and longer formal poems may be compared to 1500 to 10,000-meter performances; but Dante's Comedy is the Marathon of them all – that sustained, long run that draws on the very deepest levels of the human spirit and soul. It is perhaps no coincidence that in making this comparison we know that the very first Marathon runner (Pheidippides) completed his task for Greece, and then promptly died; it seems this more or less happened to Dante – having finished the Comedy for Italy and the Italian language, he too died very soon after. Heroic, or what?

If it's not clear already, then let me be more explicit: the beauty that we want - that our souls want - is to be found in form. Without form, there is no beauty; there is randomness, there is chaos, there is subjective whim, there is ego, and there is ugliness. Does this sound too subjective, or just an opinion? Consider then Eric Hedin's recent comment[186]: "Oftentimes we hear it said that beauty is only 'in the eye of the beholder'. But [Thomas] Dubay maintains that 'both science and theology agree on the objectivity of beauty'." In its characteristics of simplicity and elegance, beauty not only appeals to our minds, but also helps us identify scientific theories that correspond to reality. Physicist Paul Davies[187] has said, "It is widely believed among scientists that beauty is a reliable guide to truth". The great architect and inventor, R. Buckminster Fuller[188], attested to it too: "When I'm working on a problem, I never think about beauty, I think only how to solve the problem. But when I have finished, if the solution is not beautiful, I know it is wrong."

The poet John Keats - naturally as a poet might! - reached this conclusion without any research two centuries before. In his poem, Ode on a Grecian Urn, he concluded, "Beauty is Truth, Truth Beauty. – that is all / Ye know on earth, and all ye need to know." And he also said[189], "The excellence of every Art is its intensity, making all disagreeables evaporate, from their being in close relationship with Beauty and Truth." Beauty is not some idle luxury – it is itself creative and the source of creativity in others who experience it; and perhaps the final word on this is from Joachim-Ernst Berendt[190], "…one needs rhythms and meters to reach heavenly goals. Of Brahma it is said: 'he meditated a hundred thousand years and the result of his meditation was the creation of sound and music.'"

---

[186] Eric Hedin, *Cancelled Science*, 2021
[187] Eric Hedin, ibid.
[188] Attributed to R Buckminster Fuller, Critical Path and Operating Manual for Spaceship Earth.
[189] Cited in Poetry and Story Therapy, Geri Giebel Chavis, 2011.
[190] Joachim-Ernst Berendt, *The World is Sound*.

If we are to live, as the Bible enjoins us to do, we need to re-establish a new vision of the great Tradition and the living poetry without which our citizens are immersed in mendacious ugliness, and cut off from the vital springs of creativity that alone can renew us.

What is poetry's unique power in fostering human connection to memory, to the past, and ultimately, to truth? Memory, embodied by Mnemosyne, the mother of the Muses, is far more than mere recollection. It is a bridge between generations, ideas, and values—an essential conduit for maintaining societal order and resisting chaos. As discussed earlier, Apollo stands at the crossroads of light, truth, and poetry, casting away the shadows of falsehood. Mnemosyne complements him by ensuring that humanity remembers its origins, its stories, and, critically, its purpose.

Consider, for a moment, the ancients who gathered around fires to listen to poets recite epics—these were not mere entertainment. They were a method of engraving collective memory into the hearts of those who listened. It was through poetry, through the rhythm of verse and meter, that civilizations remembered who they were. The *Iliad*, for instance, was not just a story of war; it was a reflection on honour, rage, loss, and reconciliation. The Odyssey, too, served as a testament to the journey of life, the wandering soul returning home. Without these narratives rooted in the memory of past glories, societies would lose their moorings, drifting away from the shores of understanding and truth.

In this sense, Mnemosyne's role becomes clear: she is not merely the goddess of memory, but the guardian of cultural continuity. Without her, the works of the Muses would dissipate into oblivion, unmoored from context, significance, and depth. Her union with Zeus was not just a creative act; it was a vital coupling that allowed the wisdom of the past to be transmitted into the future. And Apollo, by leading the Muses, ensures that this memory is not static but dynamic—continually refreshed, renewed, and brought into the light for all to see.

But in our current age, where truth is so often distorted and fragmented, we must ask: what is the modern equivalent of this transmission of memory? Is it still poetry? In many ways, yes. Poetry today, though often side-lined, continues to serve as a vessel for deep reflection, offering not just beauty, but a profound engagement with the world's enduring truths. Whether it be in the works of Edwin Muir, JRR Tolkien, Joseph Salemi, Joseph Sale[191]

---

[191] For proof, try reading Virtue's End, a continuation of Spenser's epic, Faerie Queen: https://www.amazon.co.uk/VIRTUES-END-SPECIAL-HARDBACK-continuation/dp/B0C9SJ2TP8/

(yes, full disclosure: my son, a brilliant poet), Angela Alaimo O'Donnell or Andrew Benson Brown, poetry captures what is timeless, echoing Mnemosyne's role in preserving the essence of humanity.

Yet there is a struggle. Poetry is under threat in the modern world, its relevance questioned, its place in education diminished. In times past, poetry was central to learning—both as a form of intellectual exercise and as a moral compass. Today, however, with education often focused on the pragmatic, the technical, and the material, poetry is relegated to a niche discipline. This, in itself, is a kind of Mendacium—a falsehood that claims poetry is no longer necessary. But if we neglect it, we lose an essential tool for grappling with truth, memory, and ultimately, ourselves.

This brings us back to Apollo and his relationship with truth. Poetry, under Apollo's guidance, is not just art for art's sake. It is a disciplined practice, an effort to bring order to chaos, to give form to the formless. In the same way that Apollo's light dispels darkness, poetry sheds light on the complexities of human experience. It is not only a reflection of truth but an act of creation, building something where before there was nothing but uncertainty and shadow.

And here lies the key: if we abandon poetry, we abandon a critical means of fighting Mendacium. Without poetry's beauty, its structure, and its capacity to resonate with the soul, we become susceptible to the disorder and fragmentation that falsehood brings. Apollo, as god of both light and poetry, reminds us that truth is not always self-evident—it must be pursued, crafted, and brought into the light, just as the poet painstakingly crafts verses to reflect the deepest aspects of human existence.

In conclusion, poetry, as guided by Apollo and begotten by Mnemosyne, is more than just an artistic endeavour. It is a means of survival—culturally, spiritually, and intellectually. In resisting the spread of falsehood in our time, we would do well to remember the lessons of the ancients: that truth is often complex, multifaceted, and elusive. But through poetry, we are given a path—a way to navigate the uncertainties of life and connect with the deeper truths that bind us to one another, across time and space. As long as poetry endures, Mendacium will never fully prevail, for poetry is a testament to the enduring power of truth, memory, and the human spirit.

Chapter 10:
Kairos and Pandora: Luck and Hope

In chapter 8 we looked at the pernicious rise of Mendacium in the world today, and through the myths – in chapter 9 – we considered antidotes to this false twin of truth. We talked about Apollo, Memory and poetry as ways of countering falsehood. To win the victory over falsehood, though, we need more than just Apollo (order and understanding), Memory (recall and retention) and poetry (prophecy and expressiveness of deep truths), as wonderful as these things are. Like all major battles - indeed, like all major wars - one of the key extra elements is always going to be timing. To seize the moment, as it were; to grab the opportunities for victory that, maybe, are lying just ahead.

Time and timing were two aspects of reality that were of great interest to the ancient Greeks, and they had two gods to express the difference between them. Before considering them, let's look at what the fine American novelist, Christa ("Wojo") Wojciechowski[192], recently talked about time. As she puts it, "As we each spend more time on Earth, our perception of it shrinks... a year seems like a few months. It's frightening, disorienting, and it seems the harder we try to hold on to it, the more quickly it slips through our fingers." This is an experience many of us, especially those of a certain age, have shared.

I can distinctly recall being young when school vacations seemed endless. Six weeks of summer felt like an eternity, filled with endless possibilities, and only in the final days would the impending return to routine start to gnaw at my mind. But now, six weeks fly by in what feels like a blink. Writing this in early October, I blink again, and it will be Christmas before I know it, and then the year will be over!

This relentless passage of time feels like evaporation—there is never enough of it to do everything one hopes to achieve. Wojciechowski describes how she tried to get back that feeling of expansive time through meditation, journaling, and reading. But despite the enforced "non-doing," she couldn't reverse the sensation of time slipping away. As she says, "I did not succeed in slowing down my perception of time in a significant way." Nevertheless, one of the benefits she discovered was that she began to prioritize more effectively what she needed to do. It's a powerful realization and a worthy read, but I believe there's another way to approach this dilemma, and as often happens for me, the answer lies in Greek mythology.

---

[192] Christa (Wojo) Wojciechowski, in her fascinating blog titled "It's About Time: My Attempt to Slow Down the Perception of Time"

The ancient Greeks had two gods of time, though this is not widely known. Wojciechowski's frustration with time deals with the more familiar figure: Cronos, or Saturn as he was called by the Romans. Cronos gives us words like *chronology* and *chronometer*. As Saturn, his name is also tied to astrology and the symbolism of limitation.

Cronos, a Titan and the king of the gods until he was overthrown by his son Zeus, represents the inexorable flow of time. After his dethronement, he was cast into Tartarus, the lowest pit of the underworld. This association with decline makes Cronos a god of entropy, decay, and loss. Time, for Cronos, is a force that leads us downward, toward an inevitable end. No wonder Wojciechowski, like the rest of us, struggles to slow its effects.

Saturn, or Cronos, is also linked to the word *saturnine*: cold, gloomy, melancholic, with associations to lead—certainly not gold. Cronos, the god of measured time, brings limitations and is often a harbinger of ill-omen. In this way, time itself can be fatal, a shackle that confines all mortal beings to eventual decline.

And decline is certainly where Cronos is at: perhaps of all the etymologies that indicate the pernicious nature of Cronos (sometimes spelt Chronos), the worst is 'chronic'. We succumb to chronic diseases, and chronic means something is long-lasting or continuing to occur again and again over a long period of time. For example, you might describe a disease, condition, or pain as chronic if it lasts for more than three months or worsens over time: chronic disease, chronic pain, chronic arthritis, and a chronic shortage of teachers in the education sector or anything else! Cronos, then, has and is a bad rap.

To put this even more exactly: Cronos represents time that is quantitative (e.g. as when we say "24/7"), homogeneous (one second is one second, always the same), and secular (that is to say, everyday, mundane or quotidian). And when you think about it, this is the kind of time that the modern age is entirely obsessed with and ruled by. From the invention of clocks to the creation of 'scientific management'[193] and 'time and motion' studies to control workers in the late Nineteenth century, to the 9-to-5 working week to the open all-hours kind of culture we have now. Quite different from the agrarian societies for whom the seasons defined what time is. This time is relentless, rushing, busy, microscopically examined ('time management') and indifferent to human emotions and feelings; it is in fact, alienating.

Indeed, when we think about it, Cronos – Chronos/chronic time – also has no particular meaning, no particular story to tell, and is empty of any particular significance. In short, there is no

---

[193] Sometimes called Taylorism after Frederick Winslow Taylor who pioneered this methodology.

order – unlike the seasons – and so it is understandable that Cronos is confined to Tartarus, because all things that tend to chaos and disorder are – by the order of Zeus – imprisoned there; and one of the characteristics of Tartarus – Hell – is that nothing changes: everything and everyone is 'fixed', forever. So, there can be no narrative arc in Hell, one is trapped and there is no opportunity to escape or do anything else. Hence our natural preoccupation with those rare heroes[194] who have managed to come back from this dismal and static place.

With this in mind, we see a sort of parallel with our contemporary lives: there is lack of meaning or purpose in them, characterised by a Twentieth Century word created for this end, anomie[195]. The word itself comes from the Greek and means 'lawlessness' or 'without law' or even 'without order'. Time has no meaning; Cronos time is a material resource we use to count profit, and we spend it – waste it - as we do money; we use its calendar as a grid on which to plot inconsequential changes, for we believe, consciously or otherwise, that the past, present and future are much the same, and nothing much is going to interrupt the dream-state of our existence now. In a weird sort of way, we are like the people who lived at the time of Noah[196]: "...For as in those days before the flood they were eating and drinking, marrying and giving in marriage, until the day that Noah entered the ark, and they did not understand until the flood came and took them all away ..."

The net effect of this Cronos mind-set, aside from the pathologies (like the increase in suicide) that it engenders, is that it stultifies creativity across all areas of life, not least poetry itself. That is why – in case you wondered – 99% of all the poetry you read nowadays is not poetry at all: it is formless, disordered, ego-centric, idiosyncratic and untrue! Nothing like the great poetry we have had in the past. It pretends (so more Mendacium) to be like the great poetry of the past, and one of the main devices it uses to do so is by its practitioners also writing books (biographies, critical reviews etc.) about those great and past poets *as if they were* in their genealogical line! The websites that advocate the false poets also pay lip service in the same way: pages dedicated to great past poets alongside the false poets[197]. But I digress.

---

[194] See chapter 6 and Orpheus.
[195] Anomie, first coined by the French sociologist Emile Durkheim in his works in "The Division of Labour in Society" (1893) and "Suicide" (1897). Durkheim used *anomie* to describe a state of normlessness or breakdown of social norms and values within a society. He associated it with periods of rapid social change or upheaval when individuals feel disconnected from the collective conscience or common values that traditionally provide order. Durkheim linked this sense of *anomie* to social pathologies like higher rates of suicide, as people might struggle to find meaning or structure in a rapidly changing world.
[196] Matthew 24:37-39 (NASB) and Luke 17:26-27 (NASB).
[197] See https://www.youtube.com/watch?app=desktop&v=PKeoimeJ3Tg

If time – Cronos – is just a sequence of unrelated seconds that somehow and for some reason just succeed each other, but to no particular purpose (there is no teleology), then what we have is a cosmos indifferent to what happens. In truth, what we have is a wholly passive framework underpinning our subjective realities; our subjective reality seems real enough to each one of us, but what are we standing on? An empty clock ticking away our life. No wonder death anxiety – what Freud[198] coined the Greek term Thanatos for – has exploded in this and in the last century.

All this kind of time is very different from the other Greek god of time, or timing, that I alluded to before, the god Kairos. Kairos is an ancient Greek word meaning the opportune or "supreme" moment, which immediately contrasts with the endless succession of pointless seconds and mindless minutes that characterises Cronos; he is the god of opportunity, who represents time not as a sequence of events but as the critical moment for action. Kairos is not concerned with minutes, hours, or days. Rather, he embodies the perfect moment when action must be taken to seize an opportunity. Cronos is quantitative, but Kairos is qualitative.

Kairos was the youngest son[199] of Zeus, and so in fact the grandson of Cronos, which in a way seems entirely appropriate: from the disorder of the reign of Cronos, springs the order of Zeus, and finally the further offspring signifying good chance, good luck, the right moment for producing more right ordering – a moment in accord with the purposes of the cosmos for justice and for good.

Consider three simple questions: We've recently come out of a global pandemic—Is now the right time for a career change for you? Inflation has been rampant—Have economic policymakers chosen the right moment to raise interest rates? And finally, President Putin invaded Ukraine—Was this the right moment for him to act?

In these examples, Kairos looms large. On the third question, Putin may have believed it was the right moment, seeing division in the Western world, internal struggles with social movements, and economic turmoil. But strategically, it could have been a colossal misjudgement, a Kairos misstep, because he failed to account for the resilience of Ukraine and its supporters. History will reveal whether this was the right moment, but time as an opportunity is far more elusive than time measured by clocks.

---

[198] Freud developed the concept of the "death drive" (Thanatos) in his "Beyond the Pleasure Principle" (1920).
[199] Who his mother was is obscure, but one candidate for the job would be Themis, the Titaness of divine law and order. Given our discussion of Zeus mating with the Titaness, Mnemosyne in chapter 9, it is interesting how the supreme god needs to mate with these elemental female powers in order to sustain his order!

In the New Testament, the word *Kairos* is used frequently, about 86 times, often referring to the "appointed time" in God's purpose. For example, the moment Jesus entered Jerusalem was the *kairos*, the perfect, preordained moment for his mission to unfold. In contrast, *cronos* is used only 54 times, almost always referring to the measurement of time—days and hours. The dichotomy between *cronos* and *Kairos* underscores that the opportune time for action is often fleeting, subjective, and laden with meaning.

Kairos, then, is qualitative, heterogeneous, seasonal, archetypally informed time. It is full of potential; it invites us to engage in special moments more pregnant with meaning or opportunity than others; indeed, it is a witness to the Pareto Principle.[200] It reveals to us that there are certain times when the order of the cosmos is inviting us to act – to participate - and that our participation will have an effect on the whole heaven-Earth axis. Put another way, we are invited to become heroes in the cosmic dialogue of Earth with heaven. Clearly, Kaironic time is active, not passive like Chronic time.

So, Kairos is more than just an abstract concept of opportunity; it's a call to action. But seizing the opportune moment, much like capturing Kairos by his single lock of hair, is a fleeting and often difficult task. The ancient Greeks portrayed Kairos as a youthful figure, agile and elusive, with a lock of hair on his forehead—one that had to be grasped as he approached because once he passed by, he was bald and impossible to seize. This imagery reminds us that the right moment doesn't linger, and it reminds us of all those people who have 'regrets': a key feature being that the most common reason for regrets given on deathbeds, is not what has been done wrong, but what wasn't done at all[201].

In modern life, the notion of *Kairos* permeates all aspects of decision-making. Think of the investor who times the market just right, or the athlete who launches a career-defining performance at exactly the right moment. Kairos is about knowing when to act, and acting decisively when the time is ripe. The question isn't just about identifying opportunities but also about developing the wisdom to discern them amidst a sea of possibilities.

This concept becomes particularly relevant in our era of information overload. We are constantly bombarded with choices

---

[200] The Pareto Principle, also known as the 80/20 Rule, discovered by Vilfredo Pareto in 1896. Essentially, he found that only 20% of inputs produced 80% of the outputs. A relatively small number of variables were responsible for a relatively large number of effects: seizing hold of the right ones was the key to success.
[201] One of the most cited sources on this subject is palliative care nurse Bronnie Ware, who worked with dying patients for many years. According to her, the most common regrets include not living a life true to oneself and failing to seize opportunities: https://www.oldcolonyhospice.org/blog/bid/101702/Nurse-reveals-the-top-five-regrets-people-make-on-their-deathbed

and opportunities, but only a few of those moments are *kairos*—the critical, life-changing ones. To seize them, we must cultivate discernment, the ability to filter out distractions and recognize the truly important moments.

In a world where *cronos* dominates—where we measure our lives in seconds, minutes, and years—the concept of *Kairos* offers a refreshing perspective. In contrast to the mechanical ticking of the clock, *Kairos* invites us to live more fully in the present moment. It's a reminder that the most important decisions in life aren't always about careful planning or meticulous timing, but rather about being fully awake and ready when opportunity knocks. It is an irony of language that we need to be 'awake' (that is, to be woken) to Kairos in a completely different sense to being 'woke' today, which essentially means the opposite: namely, instead of being aware of seizing the right opportunities to improve life, we mainly stand around virtue-signalling our impeccable morality.

To go further, the Greek etymology of *Kairos* connects it to archery, the moment when the arrow must be released for maximum impact. This is a deeply intuitive sense of timing, one that requires presence and readiness, rather than rigid planning. Similarly, it is also connected with weaving: *Kairos* refers to the moment the shuttle passes through the threads, a fleeting instant that can't be repeated.

This notion of the opportune moment links to mindfulness, a modern practice that teaches us to focus on the present. Kairos isn't about obsessing over the past or the future; it's about the readiness to act when the present demands it. And often, hope is what keeps us tuned into those moments, reminding us that there is always the potential for something better ahead.

Therefore, to truly understand Kairos, we must bring hope into the equation, and here the myth of Pandora's box is invaluable. The story of Pandora is instructive in itself. In the beginning, the gods created Pandora, the first woman, as part of a punishment for humanity. This was in response to the titan Prometheus (whose name means 'forethought') stealing fire from the gods and giving it to humans, an act that enabled human civilization to advance but angered Zeus, the king of the gods. Pandora was fashioned by Hephaestus, the god of craftsmanship, under the instruction of Zeus. Each god and goddess endowed her with unique gifts. Aphrodite gave her beauty, Athena granted her wisdom and domestic skills, and Hermes gifted her with cunning and charm. Her name "Pandora" means "all-gifted" because she received attributes from all the gods. Zeus sent Pandora down to Earth as a gift to Epimetheus (whose name means 'afterthought'), Prometheus's brother. Despite Prometheus's warning not to accept any gifts from Zeus, Epimetheus was enchanted by Pandora and took her as his wife.

As part of her dowry, Pandora was given a jar (later mistranslated as "box"), which she was instructed never to open. The jar contained all the evils of the world—suffering, disease, death, and other hardships. Pandora, driven by her curiosity, eventually gave in to temptation and opened the jar, releasing these evils into the world. Epimetheus' rash action in marrying her - because he had had no 'forethought' as to what the will of Zeus might be – is really a type of human recklessness and folly: in not looking ahead to anticipate what the consequences might be. The opposite, in fact, of that mindfulness that we mentioned earlier.

When Pandora opened the box, unleashing all the evils of the world, the last thing to remain inside was hope (*elpis* in Greek). Hope, crucially, was not just left behind but preserved, and this suggests a vital lesson: Hope is essential if one is to seize the fleeting opportunity that Kairos represents. Hope becomes the sustaining force that allows us to act when the moment presents itself. Without hope, we cannot recognize or grasp the opportunities presented by Kairos. Hope keeps us motivated, pushing us to take action in a world fraught with uncertainty.

In Hesiod's version of the Pandora myth, hope is ambiguously placed inside the jar (or box), neither a positive nor purely negative force. This duality mirrors our contemporary feelings about hope. It's a driving force, yet in moments of despair, hope can feel distant, even painful. Consider the line from John Cleese's character in the film Clockwise: "It's not despair I mind; it is hope I can't stand." Similarly, the English poet Tony Watts[202] captures a chilling image in his poem Pandora:

"And at the bottom of the box lay Hope— its muffled, unstoppable cry— like a cell phone in a body bag."

Here, hope feels suffocating, like an unreachable lifeline. Yet, without hope, Kairos—the seizing of opportunity—becomes impossible. It is hope that whispers in the dark, urging us to act, to find meaning in the chaos.

Hope, in this context, becomes a lifeline. It is the force that keeps us grounded in possibility, the belief that no matter how much *Cronus* seems to control our lives, *Kairos* can—and will—appear. Without hope, we become passive observers, allowing time to pass us by. But with hope, we become active participants in life's unfolding drama, ready to take our shot when the moment arrives.

---

[202] This poem is not available yet in a collection, but for more on Tony Watts' powerful poetry, see: Stiles: https://www.paekakarikipress.com/?content=publications.php and The Shell-Gatherer: https://overstepsbooks.com/cat/the-shell-gatherer/

In this sense, hope is less about wishful thinking and more about preparedness. As the saying goes, "Luck is what happens when preparation meets opportunity," or "chance favours the prepared mind"[203]. Put even more positively, the management guru, Brian Tracy, in his book, Eat That Frog, says: "This is a wonderful time to be alive. There have never been more possibilities and opportunities for you to achieve more of your goals than exist today."

Hope becomes the sustaining force that allows us to act when the moment presents itself. Without hope, we cannot recognize or grasp the opportunities presented by Kairos. Hope keeps us motivated, pushing us to take action in a world fraught with uncertainty.

G.K. Chesterton[204] once observed, "Hope means hoping when things are hopeless, or it is no virtue at all." Kairos requires us to take the leap of faith, even when the perfect moment seems hidden. The absence of tangible evidence for hope does not negate its reality. Instead, it is a beacon, guiding us through Cronos' relentless march. Faith and hope[205] are not merely theological virtues—they are human imperatives. They compel us to navigate time with a sense of purpose. Hope, in particular, is not bound by the present; it is future-oriented, propelling us to make decisions today that will shape the future.

A final point to make here about the Greek gods and the myth is that the Greek gods did not leave humanity totally bereft at the moment when Pandora's Box was opened: hope remained, but more than that. First, we need to understand that the catastrophe occurred initially because Prometheus brought fire to mankind, which angered Zeus. Let's examine this for a moment: Prometheus – forethought – sought to help mankind by giving them fire. What does this mean?

The bringing of fire was a material aid to mankind; it enabled technology and civilisation per se. Without fire, life as we know it would be impossible. At the same time, fire is a source of light, and light is invariably in ancient texts, as we have said, not just physical light ('sight'), but illumination, understanding, knowledge and 'insight'. If you like – and again through a woman, perfect to begin with – we have the story of Adam and Eve: in acquiring forbidden knowledge they are exiled from Paradise and

---

[203] The quotation "Luck is what happens when preparation meets opportunity" is often attributed to the Roman philosopher Seneca. The quote "Chance favours the prepared mind" is attributed to the French chemist and microbiologist Louis Pasteur.

[204] The full quote is: "Charity means pardoning what is unpardonable, or it is no virtue at all. Hope means hoping when things are hopeless, or it is no virtue at all. And faith means believing the incredible, or it is no virtue at all." -G.K. Chesterton, "Paganism and Mr. Lowes-Dickinson," Heretics.

[205] The three theological virtues are: hope, faith and love: 1 Corinthians 13:13, where St Paul writes: "And now these three remain: faith, hope and love. But the greatest of these is love."

now have to face all these ills which inevitably accumulate into death. Trust between the gods and ourselves has been broken, and the consequence of this is knowledge ... and suffering.

But actually, the gods – Hades excepted – are well disposed towards us because they help us despite Zeus's initial anger. We see this in three important areas that we have already touched on. First, the role of Athena in human affairs: she teaches us crafts, strategies, and bestows wisdom to help humanity find solutions to the problems released from the Box. These abilities allow individuals to navigate life's complexities and hardships, just as fire helps with survival. Peter Levi[206] described Athena this way: as the "nurse of all heroes". Heroism itself comes from the gods – we saw this in chapters 5 and 6, and we will see it again when we arrive at the greatest hero of the Western canon: Odysseus in the final chapters.

Second, Hermes' role: we studied him in chapter 3 and focused there on an overemphasis on his technological inspiration. That said, Hermes was known for his quick thinking and resourcefulness. Though he helped bring Pandora to Earth, Hermes also played a role in guiding humanity through communication, commerce, and medicine (he was associated with the caduceus, a symbol of healing). Hermes's associations with medicine and healing (as was Apollo[207]) can be seen as a way to counteract the sickness and disease released by Pandora. His role in communication also helps people share knowledge, ideas, and inventions, fostering societal resilience.

Finally, and as no surprise perhaps, given what we have already said, the existence of the Muses is a major alleviation of the sufferings that came through the evils that were released. Through art, music, storytelling, poetry and philosophy, the Muses offer humans a means to understand and assuage their suffering, offering beauty, meaning, and reflection even in dark times. Indeed, even in the very darkest times, human beings have found solace through the Muses. This is another indirect way in which the effects of the evils released from Pandora's jar are mitigated...

And this is why all right-thinking people in the West, wherever they be, must resist all the Siren[208] calls to cut art funding in schools and education generally. If we are down to technical and 'practical' and career subjects only, Mendacium will have won.

---

[206] Peter Levi: Virgil, a Life.
[207] Both gods had connections with healing but differently: in essence, Apollo represents divine, systematic healing through medicine and balance, Hermes symbolizes the spread of healing knowledge and practical solutions, working behind the scenes to aid humanity through communication and resourcefulness.
[208] The Sirens were evil characters encountered by Orpheus and Odysseus.

Chapter 11:
Odysseus: Hero for today and journey of the soul

In reviewing what is false, we have to consider what is true, and the truest thing we know is our own soul. The worst thing that can possibly happen to us is to lose our soul; that some essential part of ourselves. One of the great sayings attributed to Billy Graham, which says this but in a different way, is: "When wealth is lost, nothing is lost; when health is lost, something is lost; when character is lost, all is lost." This soul – our true self – is some precious diamond that must not be bartered and which must be polished, preserved and cared for at all times.

Unquestionably, the apex of Western civilization resides in and spills from the Hebrew and Greek scriptures that constitute our Bible, the Old and New Testaments. Their influence on our culture is immeasurable, and we need to note at this point that Jewish and Christian scriptures are teleological, which is to say that there is an end and purpose in view and that the whole history of humanity can be viewed as a straight line from the Garden of Eden to the city of the New Jerusalem. We do not need to decide - or believe in - whether the Garden of Eden is literally true or not; it is certainly mythically true, and this is more compelling, and 'truer', than merely being historical. For as Karen Armstrong[209] observed, "A myth, it will be recalled, is an event that - in some sense - happened once, but which also happens all the time." The thing to note, though, is the straight line that exemplifies a journey.

For, it is the same straight line that characterises the greatest of the Greek myths: the Odyssey or the story of Odysseus' journey from Troy to his home in Ithaca. Yes, he gets waylaid, he gets blown off course, and yes, it is not all smooth sailing, but the destination and goal is always very clear; and it's not just a place he is heading for; it's his family, and especially it's his wife Penelope. The Bible, in a sense, is the same: excepting Jesus Christ, all its heroes get blown off course, but then God provides the correction to get the show back on the road, as it were! So, the West has this dominant notion of a straight line as an underlying symbol for how reality works.

This is important because by way of contrast, the East is not so determined: in some Eastern philosophies and religions, such as Taoism and Buddhism, the concept of the labyrinth or maze-like structures can symbolize the complexity of the mind, the search for enlightenment, or the journey towards self-realization. For example, in Taoist philosophy, the concept of the Tao, often symbolized by a circle, represents the underlying harmony and

---

[209] Karen Armstrong, *A Short History of Myth*, 2005.

interconnectedness of all things. The journey toward understanding the Tao can be likened to navigating through a maze, where one must unravel the complexities of existence to reach a state of unity and enlightenment.

Similarly, in Buddhism, the path to enlightenment is often depicted as a labyrinthine journey through various states of existence (samsara) and levels of consciousness. Practitioners seek to transcend the maze of suffering and delusion to reach the ultimate goal of liberation (nirvana). While the maze may not be as prevalent a symbol in Eastern cultures as the journey is in the West, it still holds significant meaning in philosophical and spiritual contexts, reflecting the complexities and challenges inherent in the human experience.

Returning, then, to Odysseus and our first point in this chapter about losing one's soul: how are these two concepts related? Essentially, this way: the journey home to Ithaca to be reunited with his wife, Penelope, is, on the one hand, an adventure story that has thrilled generations for near-on three thousand years; and on the other hand, it is a story of a human being's maturation. How does one grow up to be a man? Indeed, how do you grow up to be a fully human adult? And in this light, we can see that the journey home to Penelope is the journey home to be reunited with our own souls. Penelope is symbolic of the soul of Odysseus! This journey, then, is for all of us, and to use the modern jargon, it is the journey of personal development, although the phrase 'personal development' hardly does justice to the scale and importance of the enterprise.

We have the word 'epic' to describe the Odyssey, for that is what Homer's poem is; but it should be clear from what I am saying that every man and every woman's life, properly understood, is or should be an epic too. If we have not conceived of ourselves as epic heroes, then our lives are likely to be drab and stuffed-full of underachievement. As Jung[210] suggests, "when people feel that they are living the symbolic life, that they are actors in the divine drama. That gives the only meaning to human life; everything else is banal and you can dismiss it. A career, producing of children, all are maya[211] compared with that one thing, that your life is meaningful."

How, then, does Homer's Odyssey help in our personal development? First, "Narrative may be regarded as a primary act of mind"[212], and so it proves true in all great stories: they tell us the primary truths about ourselves, and often what seems to be *only* an objective narrative is also an internal account of what is going on in the soul of mankind. Nowhere more so than in the really great

---

[210] Jung, *The Symbolic Life Collected Works 18*, para 630.
[211] Maya, a Buddhist term meaning illusion.
[212] Professor Brian Cox, The Cox Report, 1989.

stories: all sacred literature, and add to that Shakespeare and Homer.

In the latter case, as we've noted, the word 'odyssey' has come to mean a journey, and one of a most difficult and profound sort. Heroes – and heroines – can only become so by overcoming immense difficulties like those depicted in Homer's Odyssey. We have to be Odysseus too. Which means - in our lives – we are on a mission: we need to get home and reunite with our own souls. These souls – which in today's terminology have come to be called our Self – have been hidden and repressed by ages of civilisation and warfare; it is to be 'home' again where home is not just an address on the door, but the place you should be and where all life is comfortable and beautiful; and it is where you find again and love 'Penelope', who is in reality not just your wife (or husband) but your faithful soul. Finally, it is where you destroy the 'Suitors' – the forces of indiscipline, disorder, chaos and evil that have been dogging your heels ever since you left home. Destroying the forces of disorder … sound familiar?

Now if we follow the logic of the Odyssey, there are nine core dangers we will face, and there are nine key tools at your disposal to help you diffuse them. What are these dangers and what are these tools to help us?

The first danger we encounter on the journey is the Lotus-Eaters: those who deal in evasion, illusion, delusion and apathy. Dreamers who will always continue to consume their lotus plant that induces this trance-like state. This state is very reminiscent of the drug 'soma' that Aldous Huxley depicts in his novel, Brave New World: it's a state-sanctioned drug that keeps the population docile, blissfully detached, and free from anxiety. 'Soma' etymologically derives from the Greek word for body – the body is rendered quiescent. One cannot help but feel a contemporary experiment in just such a drug was the introduction of vaccinations during Covid, which rendered whole populations docile and detached[213]! From this – if we want to find our souls – we must escape. The key issue here is resolution: the firm resolution to press on with the journey. In other words, the will and its willpower must be exercised.

The second danger is to become like the Cyclops, or Polyphemus in particular. Cyclops have one eye, and so they have monovision and alongside that, total inflexibility in their thinking. We remember that in order to escape from his cave, one of the key conditions was silence. Notice how dogmatic people are always talking – loudly – about their opinions; to avoid this, and escape

---

[213] This may be a strained analogy because of course it was not the actual vaccination itself that created the stupor but the fear-infested agenda surrounding it; nevertheless, in taking the vaccination people were psychologically telling – reassuring – themselves that they were now 'safe'.

the condition, silence is essential. Consider this as advice to meditate more or to be more mindful. Less words, more listening.

And the third danger follows on from the second; for it is when Odysseus breaks his silence, and exults in his escape from Polyphemus by shouting out that his name is 'Nobody' that he is almost destroyed. For in his folly, boasting and arrogance, he incurs the wrath of Polyphemus' father, the great sea god, Poseidon. If he had not been protected by Athena - through her creativity, ingenuity and help - Odysseus would long have perished and never got home. To get home, then, we need to be creative, we need to be problem solvers, for as long as we are on this Earth – and mortal – we are bound to be beset by problems. However, as we will see with the fifth danger, the Laestrygonians, we need to recognise where some problems are intractable and the only solution is to run from them!

Having escaped Polyphemus, Odysseus and his men now arrive at the island of the wind god, Aeolus. All goes well, but as they sail away, the crew think Odysseus is hiding treasure in the bag Aeolus' had given Odysseus. They covet the treasure and opening the bag they, inadvertently, release all the winds contained therein. Suddenly, from clear skies and pleasant breezes, a storm blasts them back to the island and now Aeolus refuses to help them. Through greed, they had lost their focus on getting home. Focus is the operative word: so, fourth, if we want to get to our destination, are we focused, or are we blown around by any and every emotional whim and desire?

Fifth, a less well-known danger than the Cyclops in the Odyssey, is the Laestrygonians, who are giants that nearly destroy Odysseus and his men – in fact several of his ships and their crew perish as a result of their rock-throwing. This kind of 'giant' meets us in real life in the form of problems: problems too big to handle. Often, we valiantly battle on, trying to get a grip on the problem, when any analysis, SWOT[214] or otherwise, would conclude that we should run – escape the problem by exiting it altogether. In other words, not making the mistake of thinking that continued persistence in tackling the 'giant' is finally going to wear the giant down; it's not - get real - and get out! Escape is the solution in some situations, and especially, perhaps, in toxic relationships.

Sixth, we come to the witch Circe and the drug she used whereby all the men of Odysseus are turned into swine. In short, they have become victims of their own animal appetites, and so the form of pigs most suits them. Odysseus himself could have been in danger of falling into this trap but Hermes, the messenger god, has

---

[214] SWOT stands for Strength, Weaknesses, Opportunities, Threats: SWOT analysis originated in the 1960s and is widely credited to Albert Humphrey, a management consultant at the Stanford Research Institute.

been sent to warn him how to avoid Circe's trap by eating the herb, Moly: Moly is a natural antidote to Circe's drug. In considering, then, any appetite to which any of us may fall prey, the question becomes: what is its natural antidote? The fact that we are guided to it by a divine presence calls to mind the 12 Traditions of Alcoholics Anonymous[215]: the second is Hope: Believing that a power greater than oneself can restore sanity; and the eleventh is Spiritual Growth: Seeking to improve through prayer and meditation, a conscious connection with the higher power. All processes to cure any type of addiction say something similar. Thus, believing and hoping in divine direction is not foolish, but essential. And, of course, hope is the essential virtue left in Pandora's Box in the preceding chapter.

Seventh, we come to the famous Sirens, a well-known feature of the Odyssey – their fatal song shipwrecks all mariners who pass and hear it. They were, quite literally, the 'fatal attractions' of their day. All of us have experienced fatal attractions and been driven off course as a result. The result of too many fatal attractions is a surfeit of experience – often expressed as knowing the price of everything but the value of nothing[216]. What is the cure for the Sirens? Binding – Odysseus bound/blocked the ears of his mariners with wax so that they could not hear the temptation, and got them to bind himself to the mast so that he could hear, but not respond. In fact, he was almost driven mad by desire, as he heard but could not move. This 'binding' is very similar to the Christian notion of 'lead us not into temptation' – avoidance is the key. And along with it the use of friendship – Odysseus could not have succeeded without explaining his plan and gaining the consent of friends on board who could be relied upon not to 'break' the pact. So self-limitation and friendship can enable us to survive the Sirens!

Penultimately, and eighth, we arrive at that perilous passageway we call Scylla and Charybdis. This is a particular favourite of mine and so I would like to expand it a little more. In Book 12 Odysseus and his men encounter the threatening straits between Scylla and Charybdis: there is the passageway ahead, and through this they must go; but on the left side, on the cliff above, is the six-headed monster, Scylla, and on the right side, below, there is the deadly whirlpool, Charybdis.

This needing to steer a course down the middle – or very nearly so, which we will come to – has become proverbial, for we talk about 'being between Scylla and Charybdis' – a vexatious position to be in. And Odysseus also knows (because Circe, the

---

[215] https://www.aa.org/the-twelve-steps
[216] From Oscar Wilde's play, Lady Windermere's Fan: "A cynic is a man who knows the price of everything and the value of nothing."

witch, has told him) that whereas Scylla can attack and with her six monstrous heads (with each head containing three rows of sharp teeth) carry off and kill six of his crew, Charybdis poses an even more lethal threat; for to be drawn into the whirlpool, which sucks in the waters three times a day before spewing them out, would be fatal for the whole ship and its men. Thus, Odysseus must steer right down the middle, and if there has to be a margin of error then to keep slightly closer to the left, Scylla, than the right, since the latter is outright destruction. How exciting! And this predicament is surely emblematic of life itself.

In a way we could compare the 'Scylla and Charybdis Effect' with the more familiar (in today's Western 'anti-Western' culture) yin and yang of Chinese philosophy. Here we have a concept so rich and deep that to try to summarise it in a few sentences seems insulting. But in essence, every aspect of life has a yin and yang dimension: the yin is often considered the negative, feminine, softer force or energy that counterbalances the yang, the positive, masculine and harder force or energy that interacts with the yin to create life, movement and everything else. However, the point here of making the comparison is to point out that too much yin, or too much yang, always leads to a correction, sometimes a violent and destructive one as nature rebalances itself. To be successful, we all need to keep yin and yang in balance, just as Odysseus needs to steer that fine balance between Scylla and Charybdis[217].

And there is something else in this that is very important too. For I do not think that Scylla high up on the left of us, and Charybdis low down on the right of us, is accidental either. (Odysseus is returning to Greece via the Italian/Sicilian strait, so that Scylla would be north and Charybdis south). The Greeks knew intuitively what we know scientifically; namely, that Scylla is a symbol for the left-side of our brains, and Charybdis for the right side. So, left, elevated, above us, where the logical thinking and calculation is done; the right, where the emotions and imagination thrive. We err in our lives by becoming too logical, too dry, too precise: three rows of teeth grind us to pieces, and we fight Frankenstein-ian monsters that we have put together in the laboratory of our thinking mind. If that were not bad enough, Charybdis is worse, much worse: for here we fall into the emotional pull that sucks the life out of us. We experience, as Homer put it, 'the whole sea ... boil in turbulence' and we are caught in a drag that we are never strong enough to resist, as round and round we whirl in emotional hell.

Sound familiar? Why, then, is it so difficult to steer that middle course? Odysseus was doing so well; had himself and his

---

[217] Of course, correctly understood this is another way of expressing the maxim of Apollo that we have already encountered: Not Too Much!

men on the lookout, and armed, to resist Scylla, but the sudden roar and pull of Charybdis suddenly distracted him and them, and while they stare fascinated by the great whirlpool, Scylla swoops and six men are lost. Ever experienced that? Being so logical, then one emotional fascination results in all composure being lost?

One application of this struck me when I reflected on that wonderful and original Batman movie starring Michael Keaton and Jack Nicolson. Quoting from memory, remember that wonderful moment when the Joker replaces Boss Grissom and provides (ironically) a moving tribute to his former boss (whom he has himself killed). Of Grissom, he says, "Now you fellas have said some pretty mean things. Some of which were true, under that fiend Boss Grissom. He was a thief, and a terrorist. On the other hand, he had a tremendous singing voice."! This is ironic, but there is a profound observation in this. Namely, that the Joker (surprisingly for a villain!) is avoiding what we as humans like to do: that is, to pigeon-hole people as one thing or another. We like, in short, to avoid any ambiguity about how we feel or think about them, or indeed about a situation generally; in this context, of course, sailing between – and holding one's course – between Scylla and Charybdis is living on the very edge of ambiguity.

I am British. Is Brexit good or bad? Well, personally I like Brexit and have supported it consistently. But given that, I need to ask myself, what is bad about it if so many of my countrymen dislike, detest it? What is the case the other way? To investigate this is not necessarily to change my mind (and it hasn't), but it is to keep me on the path avoiding the two evils on either side: perhaps, the contempt of the mind (Scylla) and the bigotry of the emotions (Charybdis).

Some of you reading this (and as I write it, the US Presidential election for 2024 is only 6 days away) are probably American. Is Donald Trump[218] good or bad? And, by the way, it is no good saying now that that binary opposition is too simplistic, because it is exactly such a binary opposition that most people understand and commit to – including the media. But however you answer that question, then consider the evidence for the other way. Do so, not to change your thoughts or your passion, but at least to see why others see things so differently. Are you too logical? Too emotional? What is the balance point where you really can see clearly, see clearly what is?

This is a state of mind that the great American novelist, F. Scott Fitzgerald[219], summarized in one sentence: "The test of a first-

---

[218] And as I return to writing this book, I can confirm that Donald Trump is now elected as the 47th President of the USA.
[219] F. Scott Fitzgerald wrote this in his 1936 essay The Crack-Up, originally published in Esquire magazine.

rate intelligence is the ability to hold two opposed ideas in the mind at the same time and still retain the ability to function". In other words, to steer successfully between Scylla and Charybdis. And the great English poet, John Keats, explained this in even more depth with his concept of 'negative capability'. Writing to his brothers George and Thomas in 1817, Keats said: "... at once it struck me what quality went to form a Man of Achievement, especially in Literature, and which Shakespeare possessed so enormously—I mean Negative Capability, that is, when a man is capable of being in uncertainties, mysteries, doubts, without any irritable reaching after fact and reason."

Thus, in a world that is increasingly becoming polarized, where people rush to make up their minds based on slogans, jargon and memes, the story of Scylla and Charybdis can remind us of what it means to be a hero or heroine in this journey of our life: it means to steer a straight-down-the-middle line between our mind and our emotions, and not be too distracted one way or the other. There will be multiple crises, split and difficult decisions, and along with balance, we need to develop expertise.

Finally, and ninth, we arrive at the most dangerous moment of all (outside of the descent into Hell itself) in the Odyssey: arriving at Thrinacia, the island of Helios. They are warned by Tiresias (whom Odysseus had met in Hell) not to interfere with the cattle of the sun god Helios, and yet they disobey his instructions. Odyssey is not complicit in the disobedience, but is asleep whilst his men slaughter Helios' cattle for food. What we have here is sacrilege, impiety, lack of respect for the gods – which in a word constitutes our old friend, 'hubris'. As a result of this action, all Odysseus' crew are destroyed as they set out from the island; only Odysseus survives – just! – swept back in the waters to Charybdis, where he also survives for a second time. The key faculty we have to develop here is awe: awe before the gods – a deeper level of respect for the invisible world. For as Plato[220] noted: "'"Earthly things are the shadow of heavenly realities." In arriving at massive hubris, we have virtually come full circle.

But we also need to be aware that the Odyssey points us towards 9 key powers that enable us to realise our mission in life and restore to us our souls. And this is becoming ever more vital because as Allan Bloom observed[221] some 40 or so years ago: "The quest begun by Odysseus over three millennia has come to an end with the observation that there is nothing to seek." Once we accept that there is 'nothing to seek', it's game-over for Western civilisation. Here, then, are the 9 powers that the Odyssey recommends to us on our journey.

---

[220] Plato, in 'The Allegory of the Cave'.
[221] Allan Bloom, *The Closing of the American Mind*, 1989.

First, we need to worship the goddess Pallas Athene, who is the goddess of wisdom and warfare; warfare here is understood as strategy, not as hacking others to pieces (that's Ares, the other god of war!) Athena is invoked throughout the poem, including in book 1. Now for those who think I am advocating a return to paganism, I am not; these images are, if you will, archetypes that reside deep within us and which we need to respect and consult. A Christian/Judaic way[222] putting exactly the same point would be: "Fear of the Lord is the beginning of wisdom". In short, what this demands of us is respect and awe before that other, invisible world that is above and superior to this one – whatever our specific religious beliefs are. And so, a corollary of this is eschewing atheism, materialism, and the secular spirit, all of which promote that hubristic sense that mankind is the measure and god of all. He is not.

Our second power is to seek fair friends who can help us in times of trouble. Just having survived being dragged into Charybdis, Odysseus is in book 5 washed up on the island of Ogygia, a paradise where the immortal and beautiful nymph, Calypso, cares and tends for him – and falls in love with him! He stays with her for 7 years and she offers him immortality if he will remain with her forever. The situation is complex, but two key strands of his power emerge from this. The first is that in cultivating her friendship, she saves his life, restores his power, and when he finally decides he must leave her, she helps him build a new boat and provision it. A true friend in dark times indeed.

But, also, Calypso's island symbolizes a state of limbo or timelessness—Odysseus could remain there indefinitely, away from the pressures of mortality. Her character represents a potential escape from pain and struggle, but it's also a form of stasis, as nothing changes on Ogygia. Calypso's very name (from a Greek word meaning "to cover" or "to conceal") reflects her role as one who "conceals" Odysseus from the world. Friends can do that – they can protect us, hide us. However, there is a moment where perhaps we have to leave them in order to fulfil our destiny. The interesting thing about the story here is that Odysseus is conflicted about leaving, and it is only because of the intervention of Athena with Zeus, and a message from Hermes to Calypso that enables him to go. We need the goddess of wisdom on our side at all times!

Our third power is revealed in book 8 of the Odyssey where we meet the bard (poet and singer) called Demodokos who is called to perform after the games they have just witnessed, and at which

---

[222] This idea expressly appears twice in the Old Testament: "The fear of the Lord is the beginning of wisdom, And the knowledge of the Holy One is understanding." - Proverbs 9:10 (NASB) and "The fear of the Lord is the beginning of wisdom; A good understanding have all those who do His commandments; His praise endures forever." - Psalm 111:10 (NASB).

Odysseus has excelled; Demodokos sings about the heroism of the Greeks who took Troy. In listening to his song, Odysseus – who has been at the feast anonymously up to this point - breaks down into tears of grief and thereby confesses and reveals who he truly is. His hosts invite him to tell the tale of Troy and how he tried to return and got lost. Singing and poetry, therefore, can reveal your own true nature and feelings; can help you be true to yourself. The effect on Odysseus is purifying.

There is a very revealing tale about Lenin that shows the exact opposite of listening to the bard. According to Maxim Gorky in his Memoirs of Lenin[223], he records that Lenin said: "I know nothing greater than the [Beethoven's] Appassionata; I'd like to listen to it every day. It is marvellous, superhuman music. I always think with pride—it may be naive of me—what marvellous things human beings can do! But I can't listen to music often, it affects my nerves, makes me want to say sweet nothings and stroke the heads of people who, living in such a hell, can create such beauty. Nowadays you have to thrash them on the heads, without mercy, to make them go to the revolution." In order to be a mass murderer, it would seem, Lenin had to forego – to suppress - the beauty of music, the music inside himself too, and the poetry[224] that is everywhere; for the universe means – uni-one, verse-song or poem!

We have already met the magical herb, Moly, that heals the sensual appetite (book 10); and just as in power number two, whereby Hermes leads Calypso to make the right decision, so here too: Hermes – the higher power – the god of liminal spaces – leads us to find the antidote to our addictions. When Hermes gives Odysseus this herb to counteract Circe's magic, it becomes a metaphor for self-mastery, clarity, and resilience—qualities we need to face modern "enchantments," like distractions, temptations, and deceptions. Furthermore, *Moly* can represent our capacity to stand firm against manipulation, whether it's from social media, advertising, or peer pressure. Just as *moly* protects Odysseus from being turned into a pig, it reminds us of the importance of staying grounded and true to ourselves in an era where external influences constantly shape our thoughts and behaviours. This might involve critical thinking, setting personal boundaries, or mindfulness practices.

Embracing the role of *moly* means acknowledging our limitations, valuing our support systems, and balancing personal ambition with caution. It teaches us that seeking help isn't a weakness but a wise move toward resilience. Moly serves as a

---

[223] Maxim Gorky, *Memoirs of Lenin*, 1924.
[224] It is interesting in this connection to consider contemporary British politics with a Prime Minister, Sir Keir Starmer, who claims to have no favourite, novel, no favourite poem, and no childhood fears: https://www.newstatesman.com/comment/2024/07/a-politicians-favourite-novel-speaks-volumes-keir-starmer-doesnt-have-one

metaphor for the transformative, healing forces we can access to overcome past mistakes or harmful patterns. In our lives, this might look like therapy, self-reflection, or spiritual practices. Just as Odysseus needed *moly* to protect himself, we often need our own "antidotes" to grow beyond limiting beliefs or negative experiences. This is our fourth power.

Our fifth power is in Book 11 and involves visiting the land of the Dead and invoking their spirits. Who can help you, advise you, communicate with you? This sounds mildly absurd if we think of how Odysseus does it by performing a ritual sacrifice, and slaughtering a black ram and a black ewe; in short, by using necromancy, where blood is offered to the dead as it temporarily "revitalizes" them, allowing them to speak with the living. However, even without this procedure, the dead do speak with us, especially as ideal exemplars or role models for behaviour. Ancestor worship or reverence is common, particularly in Eastern cultures, and we all hold in our minds pictures and stories of our ancestors that can inspire us in the present. Dante in the Paradiso[225] meets his own great-great-grandfather, Cacciaguida, who provides profound and useful advice to his descendants. In my own epic poem, DoorWay[226], in Canto 2: Family Scales, I encounter the presence of my long dead grandfather, and his two even longer dead sons (two uncles whom I never met) and who advise me on continuing my journey through paradise and life. But it is not just ancestors: who - now dead - inspires you? Why? Who are the models who can help you on your journey?

More briefly, not only have we got models from the past to help – which speaks of the importance of tradition(s) – but we can, if we think about it, draw on something else: our own hard-won experience as represented in the Odyssey by identifying our scar (Book 19). This is an extremely moving and private moment in the poem when Eurycleia, his old nurse, who has known him since childhood, washes his feet, her hands brush against the scar, and she immediately recognizes it. The master is home: proof of true identity (despite all the disguises heretofore), and the bridge between who he is now and who he was then. In a way this 'connection' mirrors the connection with the dead that we have already alluded to as power number five; that there is continuity and that we break this continuity at our peril; it is a form of ordering, so central to the cosmos. Scars represent memory, endurance, and the passage of time, as well as our resilience in coming through 'all this', so they are our sixth power.

---

[225] Dante, *The Divine Comedy*, Paradiso, Canto 15.
[226] DoorWay (2025) is volume 3 of The English Cantos, an epic poem modelled on Dante's Divine Comedy. Volume 1 is HellWard (Inferno 2019), and Volume 2 is StairWell (Purgatorio 2023).

Our seventh power is when we bend the bow, as only we can in our own kingdom. Here, as Odysseus did, we show our inner and outer strength and courage, and we reveal our destiny to be that person – that hero: no-one can replace us. If we don't step up to the plate and bend our bow, then no-one else can, which means the kingdom will fall into rack and ruin.

Following the bending of the bow, Odysseus reveals his true identity to the suitors: the old vagabond, the 'nobody', is the king and has returned home to claim his own – first and foremost to be master of and joined with his own soul. Thus, the eighth power is that of transformation. And one key message underpinning it is that of the martial artist[227]: "Be more than you appear". Understating your abilities, your achievements, your rank, in order to achieve several things: first, to confuse your enemies so that they underestimate you; but secondly, to not indulge in hubris, but walk with humility. There is also a third reason, which is the advice of Jesus[228] to take a lowly position at the feast so that the host insists on your being raised to a higher one; when others recognise you for what and who you are, it is far more compelling than self-advertisements.

Finally, our ninth power is our immoveable bed **(Book 23)**: the test that our own soul, Penelope, exercises on us! Have we forgotten that secret knowledge and wisdom we shared in our youth together? The commitment to that bed symbolises our fidelity to our soul. Remember at the very beginning of this chapter we spoke about 'The worst thing that can possibly happen to us is to lose our soul'? Recalling our immoveable bed is a reaffirmation of our fidelity to her[229] and the intimacy between us. In the Book of Revelation[230] God gives the faithful who have persevered a white stone with their name on it which nobody else knows; this is analogous to the private and shared intimacy that Odysseus shares with his own soul at this moment. It is profoundly an assertion of individuality; we need to hold onto our uniqueness.

We have now spotted 9 dangers, and 9 powers that help us cope with them, writ large in the pages of the greatest epic of the ancient world. In our final chapter we are going to travel even

---

[227] My own martial arts teacher, Dave Friskney, used to say it frequently, though the phrase "Be more than you appear" is often attributed to the Roman Emperor Marcus Aurelius. Though this exact phrase is not a direct quote from his writings, it aligns closely with his Stoic philosophy, particularly as expressed in his work, Meditations. Marcus Aurelius frequently reflects on the importance of humility, integrity, and inner strength, encouraging self-discipline and a focus on inner virtues rather than outward appearances.

[228] "For everyone who exalts himself will be humbled, and he who humbles himself will be exalted." (Luke 14:11, NASB).

[229] The soul, anima, is always referred to as feminine is all cultures.

[230] Revelation 2:17 (NASB): "He who has an ear, let him hear what the Spirit says to the churches. To him who overcomes, I will give some of the hidden manna, and I will give him a white stone, and a new name written on the stone which no one knows except the one who receives it."

further with Odysseus and discover that, surprisingly, there are 9 personality types that Odysseus must face, and that these 9 types represent universal human personalities that arise from the deepest levels of the human mind and soul.

Chapter 12:
Odysseus and the Enneagram

The Odyssey is the most famous home-coming story in Western literature and mythology. It is justly famous because it is a work that one can truly say is divinely inspired: in the opening few lines Homer invokes the 'Muse', whom he calls the 'daughter of Zeus', the king of the gods, as the inspiration for the poem. There is so much in the story to provoke the imagination and to touch the heart. As we have seen, this isn't just a story about a man finding his way home to his wife, but the journey of mankind in search of his or her own soul. In other words, this is not just some physical adventure, but a deeply psychic, symbolic and spiritual one too. Indeed, it is quite early on when Polyphemus, the Cyclops, calls on his father, the Sea God, Poseidon, to avenge his blindness, and Poseidon hears his son. Thus, it is that the very depths of the sea - symbolising our raging emotions and deep subconscious - are ranged against Odysseus: he must contend with them if he is ever to get home and become himself; for home is where we are ourselves. Only at home can we relax, which expressed somewhat differently is the ultimate human goal: to be at peace[231].

What is surprising, perhaps, is the discovery that the Odyssey is not just a story but also a heuristic, personality tool[232]! Now that truly is not what we expect, but so it appears to be. The Enneagram (from the Greek, meaning 9 points) is - amongst other things - a personality typing device or symbol. It came to prominence in the USA in California in the 1950s. There is some dispute amongst various experts as to the exact origins of the Enneagram but according to Judith Searle.[233] The Enneagram was known about as early as 2500 BC in Babylon or the Middle East; and that its symbol was familiar to the Greek mathematician/philosopher Pythagoras (c. 582-507 BC). So, this easily means that Homer could be familiar with the Enneagram and incorporate it into his master work. However, once it surfaced in California there was an explosion of books and literature on the topic, so that Enneagram studies became mainstream and popular around the world.

What, then, is the Enneagram? At the risk of oversimplifying, the Enneagram is a personality tool that classifies all peoples as being one of nine types. However, although there are

---

[231] Hence the importance in Christian liturgy and scripture of the 'peace of God that passes all understanding', found in Philippians 4:7.
[232] A wonderful book to which I am indebted is Michael J Goldberg, Travels with Odysseus, 2005; also, his equally wonderful, and more work-orientated prequel, The 9 Ways of Working, 1995.
[233] Judith Searle, *The Literary Enneagram*, 2001.

only nine, there is massive complexity within and across those nine numbers. So before considering how this works within the Odyssey, what are these personalities that each one of us corresponds to? Each of us is one number that has a specific self-image and positive motivation, and each has one 'deadly' sin that tends to be their Achilles' heel, and which they must overcome if they are to reach their full potential.

It is important to understand that one can only be one number, and this doesn't change over one's lifetime. However, that said, the numbers are fluid. Adjacent numbers (called 'wings') may impact one's primary number and there are other ways in which numbers interact with each other. The full details of this we do not need to consider in this chapter, since it is a book in itself! But in studying the Odyssey, it will be helpful to give an overview of the personality types before considering their manifestations in the poem. In this way, too, this book can help you begin to understand your own personality from the Enneagram perspective. As a sidebar I would add that I have been a professional management consultant for 30 years and encountered dozens of personality and psychometric tests (and types of test), and without any shadow of doubt I believe that the Enneagram is the most powerful, accurate and useful[234] of them all.

If we go round in order from 1 to 9 and describe each number's essential characteristics, it may be possible for readers to identify what their Enneagram number is. Usually, most people identify with two or three numbers, and then it's a question of getting feedback to narrow the options down. This is effectively how the oral tradition works (as opposed to going on-line to complete a questionnaire) – it ascertains what one's number is by careful sifting of the qualities of each number.

Number Ones believe 'I am right' and have a basic desire to do good and so tend to be idealistic; their deadly sin, often repressed, is anger. Because Ones are perfectionists, and so reformers, their anger is repressed for they know – if they were perfect – they wouldn't experience it! At their best, Ones are good people wanting to improve the world. Of course, at their worst they are self-righteous, arrogant and highly judgemental of others. Their modus operandi[235] is: 'Be on your best behaviour'.

The number Twos' self-image is 'I help', and their basic desire is to feel love and to be a loving person; but their deadly sin,

---

[234] My only exception to this statement would be Motivational Maps – not a personality tool – but one I devised myself and which is used in 16 countries worldwide; but critically, in constructing the product, the Enneagram was integral in its composition: https://www.motivationalmaps.com The advantage that Motivational Maps has over the Enneagram is ease of use and simplicity of understanding. When all is said and done, the Enneagram is a highly complex tool.
[235] The modus operandi ideas are from Michael Hampson's book, *Head versus Heart and our Gut Reactions*, 2005.

again often hidden even from themselves, is pride. This is surprising but arises because in their desire to help others, they often develop a sense of superiority over those they help: but-for-my-help, what a mess so-and-so would be in. Furthermore, whilst wishing to help others, they can readily deny that they need help themselves. This can perversely, then, create exactly the opposite effect of the love that Twos intend. At their best Twos are generous helpers, loving and open-hearted friends; and at their worst, they are flatterers, martyrs and manipulators. Their modus operandi is: give and care.

Number Threes' self-image is 'I am successful' and their basic desire is to be valuable, or an effective person; but their deadly sin is deceit, and often they fool themselves about their true motives. This is because image is vitally important to Threes – so as they sculpt their own image to appear successful, they can easily end up believing their own hype! Some writers on the Enneagram think that whole countries can have a dominant number characteristic: Three and the quest for success is often considered typically American. At their best they are motivating, goal-orientated achievers; at their worst, they are workaholics and, in Michael Goldberg's expression[236] 'soulless hustlers'. Their modus operandi is: achieve and lead.

Fours see themselves as 'I am different', and their desire is to be unique or an original person; their deadly sin is envy. This is because they can't help but look at others and compare themselves, and feel they come up short. Hence the focus on authenticity and originality by way of compensating for comparative deficiencies. Fours are often considered artistic types. At their best Fours are sensitive, aesthetic and profound; at their worst they tend to be depressive, self-absorbed and spiteful. Their modus operandi is: be true to yourself.

Fives' self-image is 'I see through' and their basic desire is to master, as in becoming a wise person. But their deadly sin is avarice: there is never enough knowledge, so they tend to hoard it; they have a fear of not knowing enough. If the Americans are generally expansive Threes, the Brits are sometimes considered introverted Fives. At their best Fives are perceptive, objective and wise; at their worst, they are cold, pedantic and distant loners. Their modus operandi is: think it through first.

The Sixes' self-image is 'I do my duty' and my basic desire is to be supportive and supported, and perceived as a loyal person. If Fives tend to be more loners, then Sixes tend to be more social and team workers; but their deadly sin is fear – especially of not being supported, of being betrayed. This can create massive anxiety for them. At their best, 6s are committed, loyal, self-sacrificing team

---

[236] Michael J Goldberg, *The 9 Ways of Working*, ibid.

players; at their worst, they are suspicious, paranoid and centres of deep negativity. Their modus operandi is: stick with what you know.

Sevens see themselves as 'I am happy'; to be satisfied is their desire and to be a joyful, optimistic person; but their deadly sin is gluttony, or excess. They seemingly cannot get enough positive experiences and are always propelling themselves forward to find the next one. Because of their quest for excess, often important things never get completed, as they move to the next 'thing'. At their best Sevens are innovative, inspirational and big-picture people; at their worst, they are irresponsible, shallow and under-achievers. Their modus operandi is: stay positive, come what may.

Eights perceive themselves as 'I am strong'; their basic motivation is to protect themselves and to be a powerful person; their deadly sin is lust, not just in a sexual sense but as in a desire or lust for power. They want to know who's in control and they want it to be them! Being weak is what they must avoid. At their best, Eights are high-energy, take-charge and responsible individuals; at their worst, they are confrontational, reckless and vindictive. Their modus operandi is: test people out.

Finally, Nines see themselves as 'I am content'; they wish to experience wholeness and be a peaceful person; but their deadly sin is sloth, or what the ancients called acedia - the inability to take effective action. Part of this inactivity is due to their ability to see both sides of a position, and so to fail to choose either. At their best, Nines are empathic, reliable, and harmonious; at their worst they are apathetic, listless and stubborn. Their modus operandi is: keep it simple.

Having given an overview, you might want to consider what you think your personality number is. Aside from your own curiosity, why should you do this? Well, this is a book on Greek myths, and although not myths, the three greatest Greek philosophers all agreed that self-awareness was critically important in life: Socrates because self-awareness is foundational to wisdom and virtue; Plato because self-awareness aligns us with eternal truths beyond the physical world; and Aristotle because self-awareness is a practical means for ethical living and personal flourishing! With all this weight of testimony, then, why would we not want to know more about ourselves? And furthermore, is it surprising that arguably the greatest epic in the world has imaginatively – and so esoterically – built into it, just such a device as to help us do so?

How, then, are the numbers 1-9 revealed in Homer's Odyssey?

Firstly, rather like the Precession of the Equinoxes,[237] Homer treats the 'types' in reverse order, starting with the highest number. In other words, we go on Odysseus' journey from 9 to 8 to 7 and so on, till we arrive at 1, a countdown if you will. Thus, if we consider the first big adventure of Odysseus, it would be something to do with 9 – see above – and the 'deadly sin is sloth, or what the ancients called acedia - the inability to take effective action.' Does that remind you of any incident? Of course, we have landed on the island of the Lotus-Eaters!

Here they encounter the Lotus-Eaters, who pose no physical threat but offer a "honey-sweet fruit" that numbs the mind and banishes desire. Those who eat it lose all drive to return to Ithaca. This episode reflects the modern issue of numbing out—whether through substance abuse, compulsions, or even passive consumption like TV addiction, mobile phones, or overworking. Sloth, the "deadly sin" associated with the Nine personality type, is a fatal lethargy that robs life of meaning and potential.

Odysseus recognizes the threat and acts decisively, ordering his unaffected crew to drag their entranced companions back to the ships, where he secures them and demands they row away immediately. His response shows that the antidote to sloth is willpower and decisive action, for the danger here is a life unlived, a descent into apathy and complacency. True success, symbolized by "returning home," is not just physical but spiritual, a reunion of the mind with its true essence.

The next encounter is with the Cyclops, Polyphemus, who embodies the Eight personality type, characterized by lust—not just in a sexual sense but in a broader thirst for power and dominance. The Cyclopes are formidable, self-sufficient giants with single vision, focused and lacking in spiritual or inner insight. Polyphemus traps Odysseus and his men in his cave, violating the sacred Greek value of hospitality by devouring two of them on the spot. Odysseus initially considers a direct, forceful attack, but he realizes that killing Polyphemus would be futile as they would be trapped inside the cave by a stone too heavy to move.

Odysseus instead opts for a strategic approach, exploiting the Cyclops's weaknesses: his desire for excess and single-mindedness. After gaining Polyphemus's trust with wine, Odysseus and his men blind him rather than killing him outright, using guile instead of brute force. They then escape by clinging to the undersides of sheep. This episode demonstrates that in confronting

---

[237] The precession of the equinoxes is a slow movement of Earth's axis that changes the orientation of the heavens relative to the seasons, creating a 26,000-year cycle of shifting equinox points across the zodiac constellations. We have just left – after 2000 years – the constellation of Pisces and entered the 'Age' of Aquarius: notice that the movement is anticlockwise, like the order of the Enneagram in the Odyssey.

the lust for power, one cannot rely on brute force but must employ strategy, subtlety, and restraint.

Following the Polyphemus incident, the next challenge appears more imperceptibly dangerous: Aeolus, master of the winds and embodying the Seven personality type, offers Odysseus a path home through a gift—a sack containing all the world's winds. Sevens are defined by gluttony, a perpetual craving for new experiences and ideas, symbolized here by Aeolus's unending feasting and more feasting! His gift offers Odysseus a shortcut, which should warn us of its potential peril. Sevens are prone to utopian thinking, optimistic visions that may lack grounding, much like today's culture of quick-fix solutions and technological promises.

As they sail homeward, Odysseus's men, driven by gluttonous curiosity, open the sack, unleashing a storm that drives them back to Aeolia. This event marks the downside of indulging in fantasy and the dangers of shortcuts. When Odysseus returns to Aeolus for help, he finds Aeolus has moved on, unwilling to aid him a second time. This fickle response is typical of Sevens, who are captivated by new ideas but may lack consistency or commitment. Sevens can be dazzling visionaries, yet their optimism sometimes leads to empty promises, making it crucial to approach their ideas with caution.

Odysseus's encounters—each with distinct threats—demonstrate the different ways humans can be derailed by their inner impulses. With the Lotus-Eaters, he resists sloth through decisive action; with Polyphemus, he counters brute power with cunning; and with Aeolus, he learns the cost of over-relying on fleeting solutions. These interactions mirror humanity's struggles with apathy, power, and illusion, revealing the necessity of willpower, wisdom, and discernment on the journey toward one's true "home."

In retelling the epic journey of Odysseus, we see his struggle not only to return to Ithaca but to reunite with his true self, symbolized by his faithful wife, Penelope. The journey is symbolic of the self's transformation—leaving behind the ego of war and destruction at Troy and enduring a long voyage toward inner reconciliation. This twenty-year odyssey teaches that the end goal requires a profound change from the starting point.

From Seven we move to personality Six. After six days of rowing, Odysseus and his men reach the land of the Laestrygonians, a place associated with menace and hostility. The name itself, meaning 'gathering raw hide or skin,' hints at a barbaric nature far removed from civilisation. Some critics, as Michael Goldberg notes in Travels with Odysseus, compare this episode to the Cyclops story, but he argues they are fundamentally different. Both encounters feature cannibalistic giants, but the Laestrygonians' organised and collective aggression contrasts with Polyphemus' solitary nature.

As they near Laestrygonia, Odysseus observes industrious shepherds and comments on their relentless activity, which raises an unsettling question: what kind of men "never sleep"? The harbour, though expansive, is cramped at the entrance—a subtle warning. Odysseus wisely moors his ship outside while the other eleven pass into the harbour.

Odysseus sends three scouts to investigate, hoping to find civilised men "who live on bread." Instead, they meet the monstrous daughter of Antiphanes, whose name, Goldberg suggests, means "opposed to recognition" or "unspeakable." The scouts are led to a palace where they encounter the queen, a giantess who summons her husband. Antiphanes kills and prepares one scout for a meal, triggering an attack. The Laestrygonians swarm, destroying the ships in the harbour, spearing the sailors like fish, and consuming them. Only Odysseus and his crew escaped, as his ship had stayed clear of the danger.

This disaster is worse than the encounter with Polyphemus, for unlike the Cyclops, the Laestrygonians are hyperactive, collective, and paranoid. Their aggression stems from fear and insecurity, a hallmark of what Goldberg identifies as the "Six" personality type. Unlike the Cyclops, who trusts his physical strength, the Laestrygonians rely on their minds, which are prone to suspicion and pre-emptive strikes.

Key lessons from this encounter include maintaining a safe distance from dangerous mindsets, using courage to bring hidden motives to light, and recognising when to leave if there is no chance for change. With one ship remaining, Odysseus sails on, heading toward the land of Circe.

At the Enneagram type Five, we encounter Circe, the wise yet dangerous "witch" who embodies profound knowledge but also the deadly sin of avarice—the tendency to hoard wisdom out of fear of scarcity. Fives, with their motto "I see through," seek depth over appearances, though this intellectual quest can lead to an isolation rooted in possessiveness.

The American psychologist James Hollis[238] described how a force beyond ordinary consciousness often pushes us to "overthrow" the ego. W.H. Auden[239] captured the resistance to this change, saying we'd "rather be ruined than changed." Odysseus,

---

[238] James Hollis, Finding meaning in the second half of life, 2006: "A mystery so profound that none of us really seems to grasp it until it has indisputably grasped us, is that some force transcendent to ordinary consciousness is at work within us to bring about our ego's overthrow."
[239] WH Auden, The Age of Anxiety, 1947: "We would rather be ruined than changed. We would rather die in our dread Than climb the cross of the present And let our illusions die."

too, must relinquish illusions about himself to progress. After the devastation by the Laestrygonians (Six type), where he barely escapes with one ship, he is stripped of his identity as a powerful warrior. The wisdom of the Five types awaits him now, guiding him to develop insight and self-awareness.

Circe, renowned for her wisdom, represents the feminine danger of psychological and emotional complexity—a contrast to the physical threats he's previously faced. Odysseus sends his lieutenant, Eurylochus, to investigate her domain, where the crew encounters wolves and lions enchanted to behave like gentle pets, a display of Circe's mastery over nature—knowledge that transforms and controls.

The men hear Circe's "spellbinding voice" as she weaves an "enchanted web," symbolizing the allure of technology today, where the enchantment often blinds us to potential pitfalls. The crew, enchanted by her hospitality, drink her potion and are turned into pigs. This transformation highlights the danger of becoming "pig-headed"—stubborn and narrow-minded—as their outward form reflects an inner limitation of thought.

Odysseus, guided by Hermes, meets Circe armed with a protective herb, Moly, which counters her magic. The herb, with its "black root" and "white as milk" flower, symbolizes the balance between opposites, a concept echoed in the Tai Chi symbol of yin and yang where black bleeds into white and white bleeds into black. This balance teaches flexibility, the ability to change without becoming "stuck"—the antidote to the Five's tendency toward hoarding knowledge.

Circe's enchantment fails on Odysseus, and she acknowledges his unyielding mind. This aspect of the Five types—clarity and non-attachment to superficial choices—can transform knowledge into wisdom. Following Hermes' counsel, Odysseus secures Circe's oath not to harm him, and a genuine bond of trust forms between them, a striking contrast to previous encounters where betrayal loomed.

For a year, Odysseus and his men find solace in Circe's palace, enjoying the stability of her world, until his desire to return home resurfaces. Circe, embodying the true wisdom of the Five type, guides him with precise instructions on the next, unexpected step: he must descend into the underworld to confront the deepest aspects of his psyche. This "katabasis" (descent) is a transformative journey common in myth, reflecting an inner confrontation and descent into one's personal "hell" or depression.

Circe's wisdom provides Odysseus with a roadmap, not just for the external journey, but for navigating his own soul. With her guidance, Odysseus is ready to face the ultimate trials ahead, beginning with the envy and yearning embodied by the Sirens—part of his path to personal integration and, ultimately, home.

Odysseus has faced bodily challenges—lethargy with the Lotus-Eaters (Nine) and the Cyclops' rage for power (Eight). As he advances, he faces mental tests with the optimistic Seven, paranoid Six, and knowledge-hoarding Five. Now, under Circe's guidance, he moves from the mind to the heart, confronting his deepest emotions. American psychologist James Hollis[240] noted that people often wish for a conflict-free, peaceful place—but that place is death. Odysseus, therefore, must confront Hades, symbolizing the Four personality type, to progress.

Type Four, defined by a need for uniqueness and authenticity, suffers from envy, often feeling inferior when comparing themselves to others. They may be creative and sensitive but can also become self-absorbed or depressive. Odysseus reaches Hades by following Circe's instructions, creating a trench to keep the spirits at bay and offering sacrifices. The dead are drawn by blood, symbolizing the overwhelming intensity of the Four's emotions, and he uses boundaries to manage this intensity. Fours, both in Odysseus's journey and in personality, must set emotional boundaries to avoid drowning in their own intensity.

In Hades, Odysseus first encounters Elpenor, a recently deceased crew member, who laments his unperformed funeral rites. This focus on ritual suggests that engaging in constructive actions can help avoid emotional entrapment. Fours often dwell on the past, blaming gods, luck, or others for their misfortunes. Hades, as Michael J. Goldberg[241] describes, is a place of "if-onlys" and "might-have-beens," which lead to envy of the living.

Finally, Odysseus speaks to the seer Tiresias, the "unshaken" one[242], who provides insight on how to reach home. Tiresias instructs Odysseus and his crew to curb their desires and also to make an offering to Poseidon in a land that knows "nothing of the sea," symbolizing a release from turbulent emotions. The Four, then, must transcend their emotional attachments and cravings.

After leaving Hades, the Sirens test Odysseus once more. Circe, representing the wisdom of the Five, advises him on handling this challenge. Odysseus fills his crew's ears with wax and binds himself to the mast, allowing him to hear the Sirens' seductive song, a lament that "feels your pain." This song lures Fours, offering

---

[240] James Hollis, ibid.
[241] Michael J Goldberg, ibid.
[242] Tiresias is often called the "unshaken" one because of his unwavering composure and unalterable knowledge, especially in the face of intense situations. As a prophet, he was privy to truths and futures that often-brought chaos, tragedy, or deep challenges for those around him. However, despite the dramatic implications of his prophecies, Tiresias himself remained calm, detached, and resolute. This earned him the title of the "unshaken," emphasising his steadfastness and inner stability amidst turbulent circumstances.

solace and understanding of their unique suffering. Listening without acting is essential; otherwise, one risks becoming trapped by emotional introspection.

Goldberg[243] warns that an obsession with personal pain—seeking to make others understand—leads to shipwreck. To navigate past one's emotional wreckage, Fours must establish boundaries, as Odysseus does with the trench and ropes. They must listen to their past without allowing it to define or trap them. The journey teaches the need for resilience and boundaries in handling the Four's emotional depths, for hope is essential to move forward, despite Hades' despair. Odysseus sails on, ready to confront the Three types with Scylla, Charybdis, and the Island of the Sun God.

Odysseus, having summoned the dead in Hades, faces the perils of the type Three on his journey home, encountering Scylla, Charybdis, and the Sungod's island. The type Three's defining traits—"I am successful" and a desire to appear valuable—can easily veer into self-deception as they sculpt their image to fit an ideal. Often seen as quintessentially American, Threes are driven, goal-oriented achievers but can, as we noted, become "soulless hustlers" when fixated on external validation.

James Hollis[244] observes that belief in self-control blinds us to our inner workings, a fitting description of Odysseus at type Three. At this stage, he is overconfident, believing himself in control and preoccupied with his image. His hubris is apparent as he disregards the prophet Tiresias's and Circe's clear warnings, thinking he can conquer Scylla and Charybdis by force.

Circe explains that success against these perils will require necessary sacrifices; Odysseus must lose six men to Scylla to avoid losing everything to Charybdis. However, Odysseus resists this wisdom, stubbornly donning his "heroic armour" as if he can outmanoeuvre an immortal foe. In this way, he exemplifies the Three type: projecting a hero's image, fixated on appearing in control.

Approaching Scylla and Charybdis, he tells his men the danger is like the Cyclops, disregarding the gods' warnings and glorifying his own courage. Yet, when Charybdis opens its dark depths, his crew hesitates, giving Scylla the chance to seize six of his strongest men. Their sacrifice, inevitable and unaltered by Odysseus's hubris, reminds him that some losses must be accepted without bravado.

Their next test comes on Thrinacia, where the Sun God's sacred cattle graze. Although Odysseus instructs his men to leave the cattle untouched, his attempt at "prayer" (or what might be construed as phoney piety) leads to his falling asleep. In his

---

[243] Michael J Goldberg, ibid.
[244] James Hollis, ibid.

absence, the crew slaughters the cattle despite earlier oaths. They feast for six days, even as the meat spoils ominously. Zeus, punishing this transgression, sends a storm that destroys the ship and crew, leaving Odysseus clinging to a raft. He is carried back to Scylla and Charybdis, nearly swallowed by the whirlpool, escaping only by clinging to a fig tree until the raft resurfaces.

Odysseus narrowly survives, drifting until he reaches Calypso's island, where he must confront type Two. The Three's pursuit of glory and success has left him exposed, realizing that bending rules for personal triumph ultimately invites a spectacular fall. As Odysseus learns, the cost of hubris and self-deception is high, and the path to true self-knowledge requires humility and adherence to wisdom beyond appearances.

So far his journey has exposed him to seven deadly sins: sloth, lust, gluttony, fear, avarice, envy, and deceit. Now, he confronts the penultimate sin represented by type Two: pride and dependency, entanglements that delay him for seven years! Having drifted for nine days after losing his ship and crew, Odysseus finally lands on Ogygia, the island of Calypso.

Type Two's self-image is "I help," driven by a desire to be needed. Their pride stems from feeling superior for providing aid, often denying their own needs. Calypso embodies this sin, concealing her possessiveness under a facade of love. The name "Calypso," from "kalypto" (to hide), suggests the hidden pride at the heart of her care.

Calypso, a beautiful, immortal goddess, loves Odysseus and offers him immortality and unending affection. Despite her charm, Odysseus is a reluctant lover, spending his days longing for Ithaca, anguished and trapped. This scenario, which appears enviable, reflects a deeper cultural addiction: dependency. As James Hollis[245] comments, true love allows independence, while dependency reveals the neediness of the giver, not genuine care for the recipient.

This dependency keeps Odysseus from his true purpose. The gods, who want him to grow and complete his journey, intervene. Zeus sends Hermes to instruct Calypso to release Odysseus. Hermes, a god associated with revealing hidden truths, compels Calypso to acknowledge that her love is ultimately about control and a desire to rival Penelope, Odysseus's true soul.

Though initially furious, Calypso concedes to Zeus's will and genuinely helps Odysseus without manipulation. This transformation marks the positive side of the Two types: genuine compassion, allowing Odysseus to build his own escape ship. Her gift of a double-edged axe symbolizes the potential dual impact of the Two: either to support growth or to foster dependency.

---

[245] James Hollis, ibid.

Escaping Ogygia requires clarity of purpose and vigilance, ensuring that Odysseus remains true to his mission. Calypso, humbled by Hermes's guidance, also steps back, accepting her limitations and resisting further control. This acceptance, a form of humility, tempers her pride and allows her to genuinely help Odysseus, avoiding divine retribution.

Odysseus sails onward, and Calypso, learning to give freely without conceit, moves closer to the humility that balances pride; and Odysseus reaches the last of the nine temptations on the Enneagram path. After surviving Poseidon's storms with Athene's aid, he arrives on the Phaeacians' island on the third day, symbolizing a kind of resurrection. Having confronted and overcome sloth, lust, gluttony, fear, avarice, envy, deceit, and pride, Odysseus now faces Type One's vice: anger.

Type Ones strive for righteousness and idealism, repressing anger as they seek perfection. At their best, they are constructive and principled; at their worst, they can be judgmental and self-righteous. Odysseus displays this idealism when he encounters Nausicaa, showing restraint and modesty, in contrast to Calypso's possessive "propriety."

Odysseus's journey has continually involved anger—his own and others'—and his name even suggests "to rage."[246] Yet, at Scheria, the Phaeacians represent controlled idealism, having moved away from the Cyclops' brute force to cultivate a refined, industrious society. Their king, Alcinous, embodies balance, claiming, "Balance is best in all things," and rejects "reckless, idle anger."

Yet, anger's repression doesn't mean it's absent. In the Enneagram, denial can lead to fateful consequences. Though the Phaeacians assist Odysseus and avoid visible anger, Poseidon's rage erupts when he sees Odysseus safely delivered. As a result, Poseidon turns their ship to stone and blocks their port with mountains, fulfilling a prophecy that ends their noble mission of helping others. The Phaeacians now, in fear, cease helping wanderers.

Odysseus, though, has reached Ithaca with his anger transformed. Athene, the goddess of wisdom, appears to support him openly, which she has not done until now. Cleansed of his personal anger through the Phaeacians' acceptance and storytelling, Odysseus is prepared to confront the suitors with divine righteousness rather than personal wrath, reflecting the gods' will rather than his own fury.

---

[246] The name Odysseus is often linked to anger or rage for several reasons but not least the etymology of his name. In Greek, Odysseus is sometimes associated with the verb odussomai which can mean "to be angry at" or "to hate." This linguistic connection suggests that he is a figure marked by conflict and provocation, themes central to his character throughout his journey.

The lesson for Type Ones is to avoid perfectionism, accept fallibility, and embrace humility. Righteousness without humility can lead to unintended consequences, as shown by Poseidon's wrath upon the Phaeacians. Examining one's emotions—symbolized by Poseidon's turbulent sea—helps One type manage their anger constructively.

What we have, then, in the Odyssey is an amazing journey revealing - whilst concealed in the forms of monsters and other exotica - all nine types of human personality that Odysseus faces, and overcomes, in order to become himself and be reunited with his own soul. In his fascinating book, *The Enneagram: A Christian Perspective*[247] Richard Rohr takes all this a stage further and reveals how Jesus himself in his ministry reveals all nine facets of the Enneagram. The details of this are beyond the scope of this book, but whether one accepts it or not, the truth is that the profoundest aspects of who we are can be found in this ancient tool – and the ancient Greeks knew all about it.

---

[247] Richard Rohr and Andreas Ebert, *The Enneagram: A Christian Perspective*, 1989, 2004.

Conclusion

We have come a long way in considering Greek myths and some of their impact on the world we live in today. And to be clear: for reasons of space in such a short book as this, there are many Greek myths that are equally 'telling' – revealing – and I have had to omit them[248]; another time perhaps! I am sure that the choice of gods, goddesses and heroes reflects the psychological truths closest to my own heart, but at the same time, I'd like to think that my choice is also determined by their relevance to the world we live in today. So, what, then, have we covered?

First, the importance of considering the invisible world: its psychic and archetypal entities, aka gods/goddesses. Remember, one is not advocating paganism here; but there are forces at work in the world stronger and greater than mortal beings – they are baked into the structure of the cosmos by the ultimate God of gods, aka God! But without preaching a specific religion, what this account of the Greek myths is advocating is what **David Bentley Hart**[249] is advocating (even) in the title of his most recent book: All things are Full of Gods! Glorious title! As he says, "… In fact, the foundation of all reality is spiritual rather than material, and that the material order to the degree that it exists at all (on which we may reserve judgment) originates in the spiritual."

Understanding this point has led us to consider two important consequences: one, the gods are pro-order – they establish order - which means pro-life. We looked at all the consequences of the word 'order': how law, justice, hierarchy, peace, stability and even beauty emerge as a result of order. But we understood too, that this order was not just a given but something that had to be perpetually fought for as the forces of disorder, aka evil, continually seek to undermine the cosmos and bring darkness and death. And we see this vividly today as these same forces of disorder continually strive to undermine our Western societies: the enemy is within as much as the enemy is without.

The second important consequence we learnt was the necessity of avoiding hubris and embracing humility. This is a direct challenge to our immediate behaviour, but it is also more than that: it is a recognition of a moral order that is independent of our subjective opinions, and which - if we defy it - will bring retribution. If we consider the gods and goddesses as representatives or symbols of deep psychological truths (which is one way of expressing it), then we ignore such truths at our peril,

---

[248] We have only looked in detail at 4 of the 12 major Olympian gods/goddesses, and as for heroes we have certainly not done justice to Herakles, or barely mentioned or omitted Theseus or Oedipus or Jason, to specify only 4 of many.
[249] David Bentley Hart, *All things are Full of Gods*, 2024.

because it is dangerous to ignore reality, for that is what truth corresponds with. As we said, quoting earlier Ayn Rand[250], "**We can ignore reality, but we cannot ignore the consequences of ignoring reality**". Every story I have told about the Greek gods in this book is compelling in its power and in its urgency; and these stories have survived for thousands of years precisely because our ancestors were wise enough to recognise the truths they embodied – and to seek to act upon them!

Next, we discovered that alongside the invisible world – more real than our own material world in fact – is the 'invisible' within ourselves, which we call the soul. Furthermore, finding or retrieving our souls – being reunited with our soul – was the imperative quest of our life. We – in short – need to embrace the hero or heroine's journey – or odyssey – for ourselves. It's going to be difficult and dangerous, and there are all sorts of forces of disorder – monsters – out there which seek to derail us. But they are no excuse for not undertaking this quest.

One aspect of this seeking is our need – individually and collectively – to destroy Mendacium, for the soul can only live in truth with itself. Once the process of self-deception begins, once one begins to believe, accept and promote the lie, any lie, then the whole idea of order in one's life collapses like a house of cards: there can be no reconciliation with one's soul; and no hope either for the future. A question for all of us is: am I living in truth? Do I love truth, or is truth just what I need it to be to advance my own position? Truth which is expedient is simply the simulacrum that is Mendacium, a likeness but not the real thing.

We saw with Midas himself his life collapsing like a house of cards: Dionysus was relatively kind to his hubris when he wished to turn everything to gold, but subsequently and once he crossed Apollo, the punishment of Apollo directly led to his disgrace, dishonour and death. Punishment may or may not be immediate, but what we see with Midas is a pattern of hubris – of increasing egocentricity and arrogance if you will, and a complete failure to learn from his experiences. Indeed, as small as his hubris was compared with, say, Capaneus whom we met in chapter 2, the cumulative effect of it was devastating upon him. So, we learn from it how important it is to turn away from hubris – or that vaunting arrogance and self-determination reflects a deep and invisible malaise of the soul which has begun or is advanced in thinking that it is itself rightfully a god.

And of gods, Apollo is the god of light, and so god of form and beauty. False 'things' are not beautiful; indeed, they are

---

[250] Ayn Rand, *Atlas Shrugged*, 1957.

essentially ugly, like most modern art[251] and most modern poetry. The ugliness has, as it were, the added deficit of having 'meaning' – like vitamins from flour - baked out of it. Our debased forms of art have been abandoned by Apollo, and this impoverishes people's lives as surely as it trivialises them. Writing some 20 or so years ago, James Hollis[252] observed: "Our children can hardly read anymore because they have grown up with a passive visual culture where someone else does most of the work. They have lost the power for critical thinking and imaginative interaction and are easily seduced by visual images, whether they sell products, lifestyles, or political agendas. Perhaps the two greatest addictions in our culture … are television and food." We could add to television and food, the even more addictive qualities currently of the mobile phone, the internet and online gaming!

Being clear, then, what Apollo and Mnemosyne, the Titaness of Memory, stand for is part of trying to regain our literary heritage, our sense of worthwhile role models, and ultimately to re-access beauty in our lives and in the arts that ought to surround our lives. These are key objectives and they strengthen us as people, as mortals, as societies. The relevant question to ask might be what are our educational institutions doing to further the love of beauty, the love of art and poetry, and to enable students to discriminate wisely between the meretricious and the meaningful? Ditto for our repositories of culture?

Time rushes on, and it would appear to be not 'progressive' at all, but regressive; it feels like 'things' are constantly getting worse[253]. However, there is 'hope', as in the remaining quality that stays with humanity from Pandora's Box; and there is also the little-known god Kairos who masters time in a totally different way from Cronus, or chronological time. Kairos is the god of seizing-the-opportunity-time, of the right time, of the just-in-time time! We all need to become masters of, or more exactly perhaps, apprentices of Kairos: looking for those right times when we can take action, seize the moment, make a difference, and reverse the general societal trend towards entropy. There is hope, and there is the right moment to be decisive – are we alert for these opportunities?

---

[251] As I write this in today's *Daily Telegraph*, 22/11/2024: "A banana duct-taped to a wall has sold for $120,000 (£91,550) at one of North America's most prestigious art shows, with another version of the artwork expected to sell for $150,000 (£114,460): https://www.telegraph.co.uk/news/2019/12/06/banana-duct-taped-wall-sells-120000-art-basel/
[252] James Hollis, *Finding Meaning in the Second Half of Life*, 2006.
[253] Karen Armstrong, *The Battle for God* (2000): "Despite the cult of rationality, modern history has been punctuated by witch hunts and world wars which have been explosions of unreason. At the end of the 20th century, the liberal myth that humanity is progressing to an ever more enlightened and tolerant state looks as fantastic as any of the other millennial myths we have considered in this book. Without the constraints of a higher mythical truth, reason can on occasion become demonic and commit crimes that are as great as, if not greater than, any of the atrocities perpetrated by fundamentalists."

Finally, in our last two chapters, we devote our time to considering the archetypal hero of Western civilisation, Odysseus; and we consider him from two perspectives that the Odyssey provides us with. The first of these is the nine key powers, or weapons, that we can deduce from Odysseus' travels. These are investing in the goddess of wisdom; seeking and finding fair friends; using music and poetry to reveal your true feelings to yourself if not to others; exercising self-mastery and being mindful; invoking the spirits of the great dead who can still speak with us; valuing and keeping track of our own unique experiences; becoming a person of destiny who can bend their own heroic bow; being more than you appear; and finally, committing to an ongoing relationship with fidelity to your own soul or inner being.

The second perspective on Odysseus in the last chapter of the book is the revelation (not mine!) that the Odyssey has, underpinning it, a personality tool, namely, the Enneagram. In short, in studying the Odyssey we can also dip into trying to understand our own personalities through its nine-point presentation of the types! In terms of Apollo's maxim ("Know Thyself", which in chapter 2 we have already said is more about know thy limitations rather than its modern developmental sense) this is helpful; after all, the advice given so far does in part depend upon its recipients – that is, readers of this book – being able to assess their capabilities sufficiently to enable them to act effectively. What, then, does our personality type tell us about our predispositions, and how might that help us navigate the dangers ahead?

The Greek gods saved us from chaos, disorder, and their attendant evils, and established all the benefits of civilisation that we now take too easily for granted. As we ignore their sage and moral advice (not necessarily given as aphorisms in the style of Apollo, but more as we have seen in stories, parables and metaphors), we inevitably edge further backwards towards that dog-eat-dog world that was Cronus and the Titans before the establishment of order with Zeus. False doctrines today proliferate like the heads of the Hydra: at root there seems to be the equity/equality movement[254] which seems to want to do away with all hierarchy, and which at not even its extreme limit wants to hold some sort of right to dispense existence – that is to say, all non-believers ultimately are consigned to the outer darkness, and where there is power – as in Stalinist Russia – they are liquidated. There is no dialogue; you are either right or wrong. And as for people, so, too, for statues, literature, works of art that do not conform with these flattening ideologies: abolish all that goes counter to the party

---

[254] For a brilliant account of this, especially as applied to racism, in American Universities, read Stanley K. Ridgely's Brutal Minds, 2023.

line. Against all this, and all of these, Zeus and his family on Olympus stand four-square and ready: our job, then, now to read the runes, understand that heaven is for order and heaven is on our side, so there is hope, and so be ready to act at that right time, which Kairos will reveal to us.

Acknowledgements

Many of the ideas in this book were first expressed in over 100 articles that I have written for New York's The Epoch Times. For a full list of these articles, see:
https://www.theepochtimes.com/author/james-sale

And I would like to thank especially Sharon Kilarski, my editor there; and also, Channaly Philipp, who have great faith in my work and have done a fantastic job editing my pieces and helping them come alive.

Evan Mantyk, the President of the Society of Classical Poets, for his enduring support and for introducing me to The Epoch Times in the first place.

Robert Oulds, Director of The Bruges Group, for commissioning me to write this book and for his great friendship over a long time.

Joseph Sale, my son, poet, novelist and film script writer, who has been a constant source of inspiration to me.

Andrew Benson Brown, America's greatest mock-epic poet who needs to be read in the UK!

Finally, Professor JD Wallace, communications expert, Dr Cheryl Butler, historian, Dean George, journalist and reviewer, who all agreed to take a peek at the MS and having done so, support it!

About the Author

James Sale is the creator of Motivational Maps and the co-founder of Motivational Maps Ltd. which operates in 16 countries. There have been 5 books on the subject with the academic publisher Routledge. Alongside this motivational and management work, James has had over 50 books published, including the best-selling York Notes: Macbeth from Pearson. Most recently his poems have appeared internationally in magazines and online forums. James was invited to join the Advisory Board of The Classical Poetry Society in New York and performed his work there for them at the Princeton Club in 2019. He is a regular feature writer on myth and culture for New York's The Epoch Times. In 2022 The Hong Kong Review nominated his poetry for a Pushcart Prize. Currently, James is working on The English Cantos - emulating Dante's Divine Comedy and using Dante's terza rima form. Progress on the project can be found at https://englishcantos.home.blog.

Other Books by James Sale

The 5-book Mapping Motivation series (Routledge 2016-2021):
Mapping Motivation
Mapping Motivation for Coaching (with Bevis Moynan)
Mapping Motivation for Engagement (with Steve Jones)
Mapping Motivation for Leadership (with Jane Thomas)
Mapping Motivation for Top Performing Teams

York Notes: Macbeth (Pearson, 1994- to present)
York Notes: 6 Women Poets (Pearson, 1996)

The English Cantos: 3 volumes of epic poetry, contemporising Dante's Divine Comedy:
HellWard (KDP, 2019)
HellWard (Audible)
HellWard Revisited (KDP, 2025)
StairWell (KDP, 2023)
StairWell (Audible)
DoorWay (KDP, March 2025)

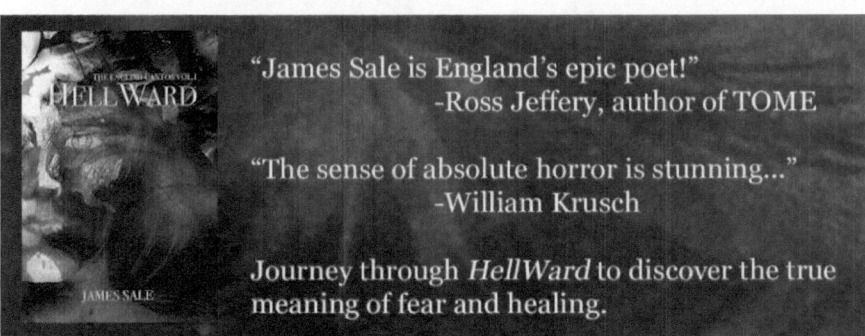

Reviews

Readers are in for an enlightening and introspective quest with James Sale's newest book, "Gods, Heroes and Us." In analyzing twelve Greek myths, Sale invites readers to explore their own personal odysseys involving the invisible world within themselves: the importance of order and humility; the significance of understanding reality through story, and the consequence of failing to seize the moment and act amongst today's forces of chaos and confusion. Sale thoughtfully elucidates on why there is hope and substance to be found in the wisdom of Greek mythology in today's world of smartphones, artificial intelligence and social media.
Feature Writer for New York's *The Epoch Times*, Dean George.

In "Gods, Heroes, and Us" James Sale challenges the common view that the old myths are just good fictional yarns. He shows us how figures like Athena, Odysseus, and Narcissus are indispensable for understanding ourselves, revealing enduring truths about justice, human limitations, and social order. In navigating the path through today's cultural complexities, we could all use a dose of Sale's wisdom—the same wisdom that has guided prior civilizations for millennia—to help us to avoid the hubris of scientism, postmodernism, and other ideological diseases plaguing our world. This book should be essential reading for all thought leaders, students, and educators, as well as anyone interested in Greek mythology and its modern relevance.
Andrew Benson Brown, writer and critic for the *Epoch Times* in New York.

The ancient Greek myths hold an enduring and inescapable power over culture, returning generation after generation to light the imaginations of not only youth, but of all humankind. What mysterious power is it that they wield and that gives them such force? In *Gods, Heroes, and Us,* James Sale pierces the darkness of time and culture to reveal the inner workings of the Greek myths and their extraordinary significance. In *Gods, Heroes, and Us,* James Sale taps into the wellspring of creative energy that has powered the greatest poets and writers of Western civilization for thousands of years — Greek mythology. He turns children's stories into a form of invisible technology far greater than any lit up screen, and he leaves this technology at your finger tips, allowing you to access meaningful ideas that resonate now as much as ever.
Evan Mantyk, Editor & President, the Society of Classical Poets.

Some of us were privileged to be enthralled by ancient Greek heroes and gods while growing up. Others received only a smattering of lore through Hollywood renditions of Troy and Percy Jackson. James Sales brings the most notable figures to life with the grandeur and cautionary tales their stories offer. This is not a children's book but rather a volume aimed at adults, sifting through the philosophical implications and present-day applications of these archetypal narratives. Sale expertly weaves mythology, philosophy, and modern-era history in a way that is both insightful and engaging. Simply put, time spent with Ancient Greek Heroes and Gods is enjoyable in the short term and beneficial long after it has been read and reread.
Professor JD Wallace.

It is often said that the Greek myths are still pertinent today because they have purpose and impart knowledge, they are timeless stories that are a source of creative inspiration. They were written however to make us think, to use reason and question our beliefs on how the world works. Like the ancient Greek philosophers James Sale has written a book which provokes, that grapples with complex concepts and challenges the reader to explore those concepts and taking, inspiration from the gods, find a pathway out of chaos.
Historian Dr Cheryl Butler

Index

Achilles, 7, 32, 46, 47, 61, 88, 90, 118
Adam, 2, 102
Admetus, 24
Aegis, 45
Aeneas, 47
Aesculapius, 16, 23-4, 27, 59
Aesop's fable of Veritas and Mendacium, 78-9, 83, 85
Agamemnon, 47
Ages of Man, 49
Agnostic, 39
Aesthetic, 71, 119
Afterlife, 15, 41, 60
Agrarian vs. Industrial Time, 96
Alexander the Great, 5, 90
Aliens in mythology, 63
Ambiguity, 89, 110
Anima, 64, 115
Anomie, 97
Antinomianism, 71
Apocalypse, 82
Apollo's lyre, 33, 64, 71, 86-7
Apollo's maxims, 24, 27, 68, 75, 106, 133
Apollo's Pythian Games, 88
Appearance, 13, 45, 47, 51, 77, 83, 115, 123, 127
Archetypal journey soul, 130, 133
Archetypes in the Odyssey, 112
Ares (Mars), 36, 46-7, 52, 77, 112
Arendt, Hannah, 84
Aristotle, 39, 85, 89
Armstrong, Karen, 102, 130
Athene, Pallas, 6, 18, 39-40, 42, 47, 49, 51, 53, 71, 91, 112, 128
Athens, 12, 14, 46
Atlas Shrugged, 13, 128
Auden, W.H., 123
Ballard, J.G., 51

Baked-in moral order, 2, 130, 132
Banksy, 72
Barabási, Albert-László, 48
Beauty, 1, 12, 17, 23, 33, 64, 72, 73, 88, 90, 92, 94, 100, 103, 113, 130, 132
Betrayal, 61, 124
Bible, 43, 47, 49, 77, 90, 93, 104
Blindness, 36, 117
Bloom, Allan, 62, 90-1, 111
Bonner Bill, 68, 70
Brown, Andrew Benson, 94
Bucket lists, 40
Buddhism (Eightfold Path), 15, 41, 60, 104-5
Bull's blood, 71
Burton, Neel, 38, 59
Caduceus, 31, 103
Calypso, 112-3, 127-8
Capitalism, 6, 60
Capocchio, 65
Capaneus, 21, 22, 24, 131
Castor and Pollux, 77
Cain and Abel (as twins), 77
Calliope (Muse Poetry), 87, 90
Chaos, 9, 11-2, 19-20, 28, 38, 42, 45, 49, 50, 53, 63, 67, 72, 82-3, 89, 92-4, 97, 101, 106, 125, 133
Charybdis, 108-11, 126-7
Chesterton, G.K., 25, 37, 55, 87, 102
Cicero, 41
Clockwise (John Cleese), 101
Communism, 6, 35-7, 72
Cosmos, 5, 8-11, 16, 20, 24, 26-8, 38, 42, 45, 51, 59, 61, 63, 67, 69-70, 72, 82-3, 86, 91, 98-9, 114, 130
Cronos (Cronus), 20, 42, 43, 96-102

Cyclops, 9, 16, 24, 106-7, 117, 121-3, 125-6, 128
Daedalus, 26
Daimonion (Socrates), 38
Dalrymple, Theodore, 16, 19, 28, 80-1
Democracy, 12, 57, 139
Dante, 21, 22, 60, 65, 88-90, 92, 114
Demodokos, 112-3
Dependency, 127
Destiny, 8, 29, 50-1, 66, 77, 80, 112, 115
Dike, 8, 13, 16, 17, 22, 61, 63
Diomedes, 47
Dionysus, 26, 46, 67-8, 70-1, 131
Disinformation, 83
Dolus (Deception), 78
Draco, 12
Dr Johnson, 48, 79
Echidna, 54
Education, 25, 44, 47, 49, 63, 86, 90, 94, 96, 103
Ego, 29, 39, 66, 91-2, 97, 122-3
Egypt, 5, 35
Elysian Fields, 61
Empathy, 73
Enlightenment, 2, 35-7, 88, 104-5
Enneagram, 117-9, 121, 123, 128-9, 133
Erebus, 9
Eros, 9, 72
Esau and Jacob (twins), 77
Eurystheus, 54
Eurycleia, 114
Excess, 13, 23, 25, 28, 72, 120-1
Fable, 3, 83, 85
Falsehood, 77, 79, 82-6, 93-5
Fates (Moirai), 8, 10, 22, 61, 70, 77-8, 80
Feminism, 80
Ferry, Luc, 67, 72
Fire, 35, 61, 78, 84, 100, 102-3
Forethought (Prometheus), 35, 43, 78, 100-2
Form, 10, 13, 15, 22-3, 27, 33, 39, 41, 43, 45, 51, 57, 60, 69, 71-2, 77-8, 82, 84, 88-9, 91-2, 94, 107, 111-2, 114, 124, 128, 131
Frankenstein, 33, 109
Freedom, 18, 38, 60, 80-1, 84
Friendship, 108, 112
Frye, Northrop, 82
Fukuyama, Francis, 57
Furies, 29
Garden of Eden, 2, 4, 5, 7, 52, 64, 104
Gates Bill, 34
Gaza, 59
Gluttony, 120, 122, 127-8
Gollum, 68
Goethe, 18
Gorgons, 51, 53, 91
Grandiosity, 73, 75
Gray, John, 2, 25, 29, 35, 49
Hades, 16, 32, 51, 61, 64-5, 74, 103, 125-6
Hapgood, John, 82
Hart, David Bentley, 130
Helen of Troy, 18, 47
Helios, 111, 27
Hera, 18, 43, 55, 74
Heracles (Hercules), 46
Hermes, 6, 29, 31-5, 51, 100, 103, 107, 112-3, 124, 127-8
Hierarchy, 6, 10-1, 16-7, 19, 50, 130, 133
Hollis, James, 8, 22, 29-32, 36, 39, 62, 123, 125-7, 132
Hope, 7, 48, 95, 100-2, 108, 126, 131-2, 134
Hubris, 2, 4, 6, 7, 13, 18-29, 31, 33-5, 45, 47, 53, 67-71, 75, 111, 115, 126-7, 130-1

Huxley, Aldous, 106
Icarus, 26
Illusions, 32, 123-4
Inferno, 21-2, 65, 89-90, 114
Inflation, 69, 98
Information, 56-7, 83, 99
Integrity, 44, 115
Internet, 32, 85, 132
Invisibility, 4, 51
Ithaca, 39, 104-5, 121-2, 127-8
James, Clive, 65
Jason and the Argonauts, 46, 130
Jesus Christ, 23, 44, 70, 99, 104, 129
Jones, Peter, 20
Johnson, Bryan, 60
Justice, 1, 5, 8, 10-1, 13-5, 17, 20, 22, 25, 36, 38, 42, 45, 48
Jung, Carl, 10, 22, 61, 105
Kairos, 7, 95, 98-102, 132, 134
Keats, John, 92, 111
King Laius, 29
Knowledge, 2-5, 12, 28-9, 41-2, 44, 64-5, 84, 86, 91, 102-3, 112, 115, 119, 123-5, 127
Kruk, Edward, 19
Laestrygonians, 107, 122-4
LaFave, Kenneth, 16
Lake Lerna, 54
Law, 5, 10-7, 21, 29, 34, 38, 49, 55, 61, 63, 70, 97-8, 130
Leto, 26
Levi-Strauss, Claude, 11
Liberty, 38, 50
Longevity, 49
Lot's wife, 65
Lotus-Eaters, 106, 121-2, 125
Luck, 7, 31, 95, 98, 102, 125
Marlborough, Duke of, 90-1
Marx, Karl, 5
Marxism, 37

Mendacium (Falsehood), 6, 77, 79-86, 88, 94-5, 97, 103, 131
Menelaus, 18, 47
Mercury, 28-9
Midas, 6, 26, 53, 67-73, 77, 131
Mnemosyne (Memory), 86-7, 93-4, 98, 132
Money, 17, 28, 31, 36, 60, 64, 68-70, 72, 97
Moirai (Fates), See Fates
Moralitis, 22, 81
Morality, 5, 14, 16, 37-8, 41-2, 100
Mount Olympus, 60
Mount Sipylus, 26
Muir, Edwin, 93
Muses, 86-8, 90, 93, 103
Narrative, 3, 50, 77, 97, 105
NASA, 34
Narcissism, 73, 75
Nemesis, 8, 22, 35, 61, 75
Nieboer, Jeremy, 34
Niobe, 26
Nyx, 9
O'Donnell, Angela Alaimo, 94
Oedipus, 8, 18, 29, 34, 37, 130
Orpheus, 6, 59, 63-7, 77, 84, 97, 103
Orwell, George, 38
Pandora, 7, 95, 100-3
Paglia, Camille, 80
Paris, 18
Pascal's Wager, 41
Penelope, 39, 50, 104-6, 115, 122, 127
Persephone, 64
Perseus, 6, 46, 49-54, 65, 67, 91
Peterson, Jordan B., 6, 16, 73, 81
Philosophy, 2, 13, 49, 55, 103-4, 109, 115
Plato, 12-4, 72, 75, 113, 120
Pluto, 61, 64

Poetry, 7, 23, 33, 63-4, 84, 86-8, 90-5, 97, 101, 103, 115, 132-3
Pol Pot, 38
Popper, Karl, 37
Poseidon, 39, 46-7, 53, 107, 117, 125, 128
Progress, 2-4, 25, 29, 49, 55, 63, 124-5
Prometheus, 35-6, 43, 78, 84, 100, 102
Prophecy, 7, 9, 23, 29, 34, 43, 86-8, 95, 128
Psychopompos, 32
Queen Jocasta, 29
Reality, 1, 3-5, 13, 16, 22-3, 38, 44, 52, 59-62, 65-6, 75, 78, 83, 85, 91-2, 95, 98, 102, 104, 106, 130-1
Righteousness, 128-9
Sagan, Carl, 56
Sale, Joseph, 93
Salemi, Joseph, 93
Tao Te Ching, 1, 4, 11, 25, 69-70, 80, 104
Titans, 9-11, 16, 20, 24, 42-3, 46, 61, 78, 87, 133
Tolkien, J.R.R., 57, 93
Trojan, 46-7, 52
Troy, 18, 47, 52, 104, 113, 122
Underworld, 54, 61, 65, 74, 84, 96, 124
Warhol, Andy, 72
Virtue, 28, 38, 48, 75, 77, 100, 102, 108, 120
Virtue's End, 93
Yeats, WB, 86

THE BRUGES GROUP

The Bruges Group is an independent all-party think tank. Set up in 1989, its founding purpose was to resist the encroachments of the European Union on our democratic self-government. The Bruges Group spearheaded the intellectual battle to win a vote to leave the European Union and against the emergence of a centralised EU state. With personal freedom at its core, its formation was inspired by the speech of Margaret Thatcher in Bruges in September 1988 where the Prime Minister stated, "We have not successfully rolled back the frontiers of the State in Britain only to see them re-imposed at a European level."

We now face a more insidious and profound challenge to our liberties – the rising tide of intolerance. The Bruges Group challenges false and damaging orthodoxies that suppress debate and incite enmity. It will continue to direct Britain's role in the world, act as a voice for the Union, and promote our historic liberty, democracy, transparency, and rights. It spearheads the resistance to attacks on free speech and provides a voice for those who value our freedoms and way of life.

WHO WE ARE

Founder President:
The Rt Hon. The Baroness Thatcher of Kesteven LG, OM, FRS

Chairman:
Barry Legg

Director:
Robert Oulds MA, FRSA

Washington D.C. Representative:
John O'Sullivan CBE

Founder Chairman:
Lord Harris of High Cross

Former Chairmen:
Dr Brian Hindley, Dr Martin Holmes & Professor Kenneth Minogue

Academic Advisory Council:
Professor Tim Congdon
Dr Richard Howarth
Professor Patrick Minford
Andrew Roberts
Martin Howe, KC
John O'Sullivan, CBE

Sponsors and Patrons:
E P Gardner Dryden
Gilling-Smith
Lord Kalms
David Caldow
Andrew Cook
Lord Howard
Brian Kingham
Lord Pearson of Rannoch
Eddie Addison
Ian Butler
Thomas Griffin
Lord Young of Graffham
Michael Fisher
Oliver Marriott
Hon. Sir Rocco Forte
Michael Freeman
Richard E.L. Smith

MEETINGS

The Bruges Group holds regular high-profile public meetings, seminars, debates, and conferences. These enable influential speakers to contribute to the European debate. Speakers are selected purely by the contribution they can make to enhance the debate.

For further information about the Bruges Group, to attend our meetings, or join and receive our publications, please see the membership form at the end of this paper. Alternatively, you can visit our website www.brugesgroup.com or contact us at info@brugesgroup.com.

Contact us
For more information about the Bruges Group please contact:
Robert Oulds, Director
The Bruges Group, 246 Linen Hall, 162-168 Regent Street, London W1B 5TB
Tel: +44 (0)20 7287 4414 Email: info@brugesgroup.com

www.brugesgroup.com

www.ingramcontent.com/pod-product-compliance
Lightning Source LLC
Chambersburg PA
CBHW060451080526
44584CB00015B/1407